westermann

CAMDEN TOWN

Oberstufe

Arbeitsheft zu den Pflichtmaterialien

Erarbeitet von

Svenja Alpen-Kühne
Florian Brauel
Ilka Kratz
Alexander Kuhrs Woltin
Jana Oldendörp

Abkürzungen:

AE	American English	*infml.*	informal
BE	British English	*pl.*	plural
e.g.	exempli gratia (Latin) = for example	*sb*	somebody
i.e.	id est (Latin) = that is	*sth*	something

Webcodes
Auf manchen Seiten findest du Webcodes, die dich zu zusätzlichen Materialien im Internet führen. Gib dazu einfach den Code auf www.westermann.de/webcode ins Suchfeld ein.

Filmauszüge
Je nach Abspielgerät und verwendeter Software kann es vorkommen, dass die Zeitangaben zu den Filmauszügen nicht exakt mit den im Kapitel angegebenen übereinstimmen.

Greetings from Bury Park
Die Verweise zu *Greetings from Bury Park* beziehen sich auf die Ausgabe Sarfraz Manzoor, *Greetings from Bury Park* (ISBN: 978-3-425-73071-4), die bei Westermann erhältlich ist.
Kostenlose Annotationen können auf www.westermann.de heruntergeladen werden.

seven methods of killing kylie jenner
Die Verweise zu *seven methods of killing kylie jenner* beziehen sich auf die Ausgabe Jasmine Lee-Jones, *seven methods of killing kylie jenner* (ISBN: 978-3-425-73070-7), die bei Westermann erhältlich ist.
Kostenlose Annotationen können auf www.westermann.de heruntergeladen werden.

Verweise auf *Skills pages* und *Workshops*
Die Verweise auf *Skills pages* und *Workshops* beziehen sich auf das Schülerbuch *Camden Town Oberstufe Qualifikationsphase Niedersachsen*, ISBN: 978-3-425-73642-6.

Druck A[1] / Jahr 2023
Alle Drucke der Serie A sind im Unterricht parallel verwendbar.

Redaktion: Dr. Stephanie Kramer, Leah Wildner
Umschlaggestaltung: Gingco.Net Werbeagentur GmbH & Co. KG, Braunschweig
Layout: Visuelle Lebensfreude, Hannover; thom bahr GRAFIK, Mainz
Druck und Bindung: Westermann Druck GmbH, Georg-Westermann-Allee 66, 38104 Braunschweig

ISBN 978-3-425-**73685**-3

Contents

			Abiturvorgaben / Themen
133		**Post-reading**: Relationships • Characterization • Illustrations and graphic layout of the play's script • Putting the play on stage • VIPs • Body images • Elements and structure of a play • Reviews	Gender and sexual diversity
138	Topic	**The influence of social media on young people's identity**	Ethnic identity The Media
140		**The role of ethnic identity on (social) media** Stating your opinion • Mediation • Cartoon analysis – images of black female identity • Looking back at the play	The influence of social media on public opinion and personal life Gender Ethnic diversity

Liebe Schülerin, lieber Schüler,
mit diesem Arbeitsheft kannst du dich ideal auf das Abitur vorbereiten. Du beschäftigst dich mit allen Texten und Filmen, die für das Abitur vorgeschrieben sind, und außerdem mit weiteren abiturrelevanten Themen. Für das schriftliche Abitur 2025 müssen die folgenden Materialien unter den genannten inhaltlichen Gesichtspunkten behandelt werden:

Autobiographie:
Sarfraz Manzoor, *Greetings from Bury Park* (2008)
➡ verbindliche Unterrichtsaspekte:
- growing up
- (ethnic) identity
- Britishness and multicultural Britain

Short stories:
Camille Acker, *Cicada* (2018)
Nafissa Thompson-Spires, *Fatima, the Biloquist: A Transformation Story* (2018)
➡ verbindliche Unterrichtsaspekte:
- ethnic identity
- discrimination

Film:
Pride (Matthew Warchus, 2014)
➡ verbindliche Unterrichtsaspekte:
- coming of age
- sexual diversity
- tolerance and discrimination

Film (Berufliche Gymnasien):
The Founder (John Lee Hancock, 2016)
➡ verbindliche Unterrichtsaspekte:
- American Dream
- ethics in the world of business

Kurzdrama (Allgemein bildende Schulen):
Jasmine Lee-Jones, *seven methods of killing kylie jenner* (2021)
➡ verbindliche Unterrichtsaspekte:
- ethnic identity
- the influence of social media on personal life and public opinion

Aufbau des Arbeitshefts

Vor der Lektürearbeit werden in **Part 1**: *Greetings from Bury Park* auf *Topic-Seiten* erste für die Erarbeitung relevante thematischen Aspekte (Abitur- und Lehrplanvorgaben) eingeführt. Danach erfolgt eine inhaltliche Sicherung und allgemeine Bearbeitung. Im weiteren Kapitelverlauf werden die Lehrplanvorgaben auf zusätzlichen *Topic-Seiten* generell behandelt, bevor sie im Kontext des Textes noch einmal vertieft werden.
In **Part 2**: *Black American female experience(s)* wird mit *Topic-Seiten* begonnen, bevor dann die beiden Kurzgeschichten im Fokus stehen. Eine verlgeichende Betrachtung beider Texte rundet die Analysen ab.
In **Part 3**, **4** und **5** erfolgt zunächst die Arbeit mit den Pflichtmaterialien, bevor dann die bereits in den Übungen aufgegriffenen relevanten thematischen Aspekte auf *Topic-Seiten* vertieft werden.

An vielen Stellen findest du interne Verweise auf *Language support* in diesem Heft sowie Verweise auf *Skills pages* und *Workshops* im Schülerbuch *Camden Town Oberstufe Qualifikationsphase* (ISBN: 978-3-425-73642-6). Die *Skills pages* geben dir Hilfestellungen zu wichtigen Aufgabenformaten. In den *Workshops* werden bestimmte Kompetenzen intensiv trainiert. Im Schülerbuch werden außerdem weitere Aspekte der Themen dieses Arbeitsheftes behandelt.

Historical background on the British Empire: "The sun never sets on the British Empire"

1

a) Look at the map below and list the countries that belonged to the British Empire. For a larger image, use the webcode. **Webcode DSW-73685-01**

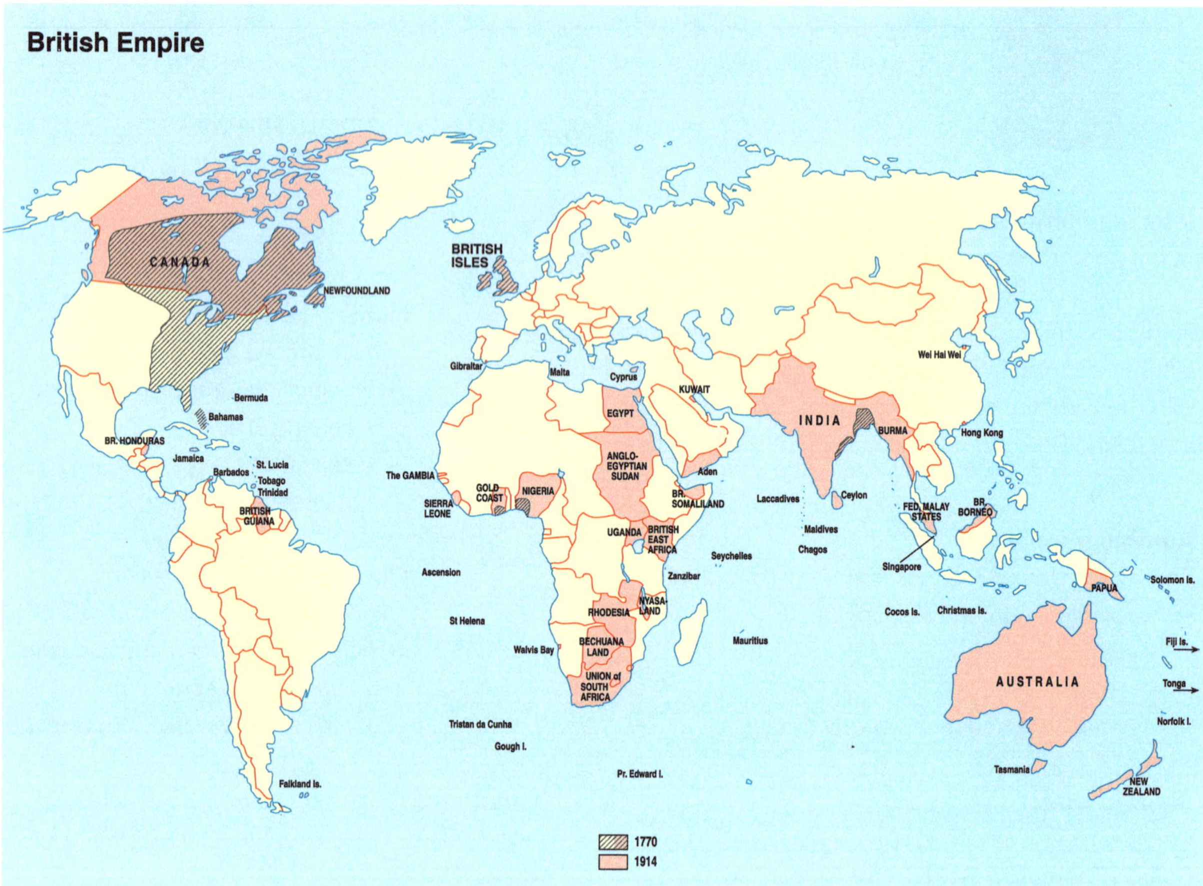

____

____

b) **Milling around**: Give a two-minute talk on one of the following countries that belonged to the British Empire, in which you outline the country's colonial past. Refer to the beginning and end of colonialism in that country. → **Language support** Giving a presentation, p. 115

Canada | India | Australia | Nigeria | Egypt | Burma / Myanmar | Ireland | Sudan | Kenya | Malaya / Malaysia | Jamaica | Cyprus | Hong Kong | Pakistan

c) Explain the quote: "The sun never sets on the British Empire" with reference to the map and the talks you have listened to.

IMMIGRATION TO BRITAIN

After World War II a worldwide process of decolonization set in, in which Britain granted its colonies independence. In the aftermath England has become a country of immigration for the people from its former colonies, now called the Commonwealth.

2

Read the text about immigration to Britain. The passages have all been jumbled up. Put them into the correct chronological order.

1	2	3	4	5	6	7	8	9	10
c)									

a) Immigration from the West Indies was encouraged by the British Nationality Act of 1948, which gave all Commonwealth citizens free entry into Britain, and by a tough new US immigration law introduced in 1952, which restricted entry into the USA. The symbolic starting point of this mass migration to the 'mother country' was the journey of the SS Empire Windrush from Kingston, Jamaica, to Tilbury, Essex, in June 1948. On board were almost 500 West Indians intent on starting new lives in Britain.

b) The Race Relations Amendment Act of 2000 was introduced as a result of the Stephen Lawrence Inquiry of 1999. This was held in response to the campaigning of the black community following the flawed investigation of the murder of black teenager Stephen Lawrence in 1993. The inquiry's report acknowledged the existence of 'institutional racism' in the police and other organisations. The Scarman Report, produced as a result of unrest in Brixton, south London and other urban areas in 1981, also called for reform.

c) When the Second World War ended in 1945, it was quickly recognised that the reconstruction of the British economy required a large influx of immigrant labour. The Royal Commission on Population reported in 1949 that immigrants of 'good stock' would be welcomed 'without reserve', and potential newcomers from the Caribbean and elsewhere soon became aware of the pressing needs of the labour market in the UK.

d) Since the 1960s Britain has developed a substantial body of race relations legislation. Various Race Relations Acts (1965, 1968, 1976 and 2000) have provided a statutory basis for stamping out racial discrimination in employment and other areas. To reinforce this legislation, organisations such as the Commission for Racial Equality (created as part of the 1976 Race Relations Act) have tried to ensure that the principle of racial equality is put into practice.

e) The majority of immigrants from the Indian subcontinent arrived in Britain during the 1950s and 1960s. Although often lumped together as one group by white Britons, these newcomers, in fact, came from a variety of backgrounds. They included Hindus from the Gujarat region of western India, Sikhs from the eastern Punjab region, and Muslims both from the west part of Pakistan and from East Pakistan, which became Bangladesh in 1971.

f) In the 21st century, Britain is a multi-racial society. The huge contributions made by the various immigrant communities to Britain's economic and social development since the Second World War are now widely recognised. Their role in creating a more diverse and tolerant society is indisputable.

g) The appeal for new workers was, however, aimed primarily at white Europeans, who had dominated immigration to Britain during the century before the Second World War and still played an important role after 1945. Even in the 1970s, the Irish remained the largest immigrant community in Britain. In the years immediately after the war, new arrivals came from all over Europe. These included a small number of German prisoners of war, a larger number of refugees from the Communist regimes in Eastern Europe and the Soviet Union (130,000 Poles arrived during the first few years after the war, and 14,000 Hungarians after the failure of the 1956 uprising in Hungary), substantial numbers of Irish and Italian labourers, and a wide variety of displaced persons from refugee camps throughout Europe.

h) Assessing how these immigrants have been welcomed in Britain since the 1950s is a complicated task. There was, and still is, a minority of hardcore racists, with policies based on the idea of 'keeping Britain white' and banning all immigration. Groups such as the British National Party (BNP) have remained on the extremist fringe of British politics. It is also true that black and Asian immigrants faced various degrees of hostility and racial prejudice in postwar Britain. Surveys conducted in the mid-1960s, for example, revealed that four out of five British people felt that 'too many immigrants had been let into the country'.

i) Postwar immigration also attracted, for the first time, large numbers of workers and their families from outside Europe – mainly from the Caribbean and from India and Pakistan (the two separate states created by 'partition' after Britain relinquished its Indian empire in 1947). During the 1950s in particular, Britain's non-white immigrant population increased rapidly in size.

j) This view has expressed itself relatively rarely in racist violence – the flashpoints in Britain during the past 50 years have largely been confined to poor areas where local white and black communities compete for scarce jobs and housing. But it has frequently been represented by more casual and insidious forms of racism. Anti-immigrant feelings have also been inflamed, both directly and indirectly, by agitation for tighter immigration controls – usually proposed when there is not an acute labour shortage.

A timeline

3

a) Scan the texts from the previous task for historical facts and draw a timeline to show when and why immigrants have come to Britain.

time	1939–45 WWII
country of origin	
reasons for immigration	

time	1945–2000
country of origin	
reasons for immigration	

b) **Pair work** Talk to your partner: What do you find striking?

PRE-READING

Musical background: Bruce Springsteen

1

a) Find out information about Bruce Springsteen. Use the mind map below.
b) **Pair work** Then share your information with a partner and add new pieces to your list. One field is left for additional notes.

his nickname and its origin:

his childhood and education:

date and place of birth:

career, kind of music:

number of songs / most famous:

themes of his songs:

his relationship to his parents:

c) **Group work** Divide the class into 9 groups. Each group deals with one of the songs composed by Bruce Springsteen that headline each chapter of the memoir. You can download your group's individual worksheet here: **Webcode** **DSW-73685-02** and the lyrics here: **Webcode** **DSW-73685-03**. Do the tasks on your sheet.

d) **Group work** Place a sheet of paper lengthwise and copy the grid on the right.
- Outline your song's lyrics in 1-2 sentences.
- State the theme of the song.
- Copy a line that you find the most interesting and explain your choice.
- You will need the last line called *Relevance* in the post-reading section for task 41.

song:	"My father's house"	...
outline:		
theme:		
line:		
relevance for Sarfraz Manzoor:		

e) **Group work** Form new expert groups with an expert on each song. Present your findings and complete your grid.

WHILE READING

Info

Keeping a reading journal will help you follow and keep track of all the different aspects the author talks about in his memoirs. The journal will make it easier for you to understand the structure of the memoirs and the issues it deals with. Initial responses to the text or questions can be noted down in the section "My notes". As the memoirs do not have a linear structure, you can also note down time markers for your orientation in the section "The setting". You should take notes in the simple present.

2

Copy the template on an A4 piece of paper. While reading the book, take notes on what you consider most important for each section.

(Sarfraz Manzoor) ***Greetings from Bury Park*** *(2007)*		
Chapter:		***Important new words:***
Topics / Issues:	***Characters:***	***Setting (time and place):***
		My notes:

FOCUS ON CHAPTER 1: MY FATHER'S HOUSE

3

Read the chapter. Then check if the statements below are right or wrong. Give evidence or correct them, if necessary.

	statement	evidence / correction	right	wrong
0	Sarfraz dresses as a punk in the 1990s.	*"shoulder-length dreadlocks, a silver nose ring" (p. 44), "black leather trousers" (p. 45)*		✓
1	Sarfraz worked for many companies before he became a full-time journalist.			
2	His father does not approve of Sarfraz becoming a journalist.			
3	Sarfraz enjoys the interview with Elizabeth Wurtzel.			
4	Sarfraz describes himself as a British Pakistani.			
5	Mohammed Manzoor spent two years in Britain before his young family from Pakistan joined him.			
6	The family spent their first years in Britain in a respectable residential area.			

	statement	evidence / correction	right	wrong
7	Mohammed is too workshy to work extra shifts to make ends meet.			
8	The whole family must contribute to the family's income.			
9	The Manzoor family adapts to the British lifestyle.			
10	Mohammed helps other Pakistanis to settle in England.			

The Manzoor family

4

a) Collect information about the members of the Manzoor family in England and Pakistan in your reading journal and start a family tree below. Add information about the family while you read along.

Tip You can find language support on the topic Talking about people and relationships in *Camden Town Oberstufe* on page 187.

b) Choose one member (Mohammed, Rasool Bibi, Navela, Sohail, Sarfraz or Uzma) and take notes on his or her development in your reading journal while reading.

c) Examine the roles the members of the family play and the duties they have to fulfill.

Making a living in England

5

a) Find information about Mohammed Manzoor's (working) life in England. Use the grid below for your notes.

Tip Use your reading journal to find information more easily.

the beginnings:	
his early years with his family:	
middle age:	
his retirement:	

b) Describe the role Rasool Bibi and Navela play for the Manzoor family in making ends meet.

___

___

c) Explain what Sohail means when he tells Sarfraz: "Go, try to succeed. I will keep things going here. [...] We will all work harder to give you the chance to make it." *(p. 51)*

d) **Group work (5)** Each group member steps into the shoes of one of the following Manzoor family members: Mohammed, Rasool Bibi, Navela, Sohail or Sarfraz.
Write an interior monologue in which you reflect upon your role within this family. Consider ...
- how you contribute to the family's income.
- what dreams you had / have for yourself.
- what you want(ed) to achieve.
- how you feel about your role.

Present your monologue to the group.

Tip You can find tips for the appropriate language and content when writing an interior monologue in *Camden Town Oberstufe* on page 319 3b) as well as on p. 332 B.

Children

6

When Mohammed Sadiq pays Mohammed Manzoor a visit, they talk about the role of one's children. Read the following passage: "'Is a cup of tea possible?' my father asked my mother [...] The only other thing they had in common was children." *(p. 23, l. 17 to p. 25, l. 28)*

a) Read the sentence halves and complete them. Give evidence from the text.

	statements	evidence
1.	Sadiq wants to know if Sohail and Navela ...	
2.	Sadiq realises that for the Manzoors moving to a white residential area ...	
3.	Sadiq thinks that children should ...	
4.	Sadiq fears that Pakistani children become ...	
5.	Sadiq believes that sending the children to their families in Pakistan helps them to ...	
6.	Manzoor does not want his children to ...	
7.	Manzoor's friends remind him of ...	

b) Analyse how the Pakistanis in the book view the influence of white people on their children.
c) **Group work** Discuss to what extent Mohammed Manzoor differs from Mr Sadiq's attitude.

Father and son

7

a) Explain what Sarfraz means when he says: "I am pleased my father smoked; glad that there were some things he did purely for pleasure and only for himself." *(p. 22)*

What does this reveal about Sarfraz's attitude towards his father?

b) **Think-Pair-Share**
Think Choose adjectives from the box that best describe the relationship between Sarfraz and Mohammed and give evidence from the text.

affectionate | cold | difficult | fragile | friendly | happy | harmonious | indifferent | intense | intimate | joyful | obsessive | poor | respectful | stable | strong | tense | uninterested

Pair Discuss if the relationship changes or stays the same over the years. Consider the following quote:

"The one person whose approval means most to me is unable to grant it. Where once it was resentment which inspired me, now it is the hope that in my own life I can do his memory proud. These days I am a willing prisoner of my father's house." *(p. 54)*

Share Exchange your ideas in class.

c) Read the following excerpt and outline the situation *(p. 44, ll. 9-25)*.

d) **Group work (3)** Imagine you are Mohammed, Rasool Bibi and Sarfraz. Use the thought bubbles below to write what they might be thinking at this moment.

Mohammed	Rasool Bibi	Sarfraz

Values

8

a) Read the following extract *(p. 26, l. 13 to p. 27, l. 27)* and analyse the values that are expressed.

b) Explain why Sarfraz mocks the values his father holds.

Language support

In the extract Sarfraz Manzoor describes the values his father holds onto. Above all, the author recognizes that his father has a stable moral framework. This can be seen in line … when he says "…" |
Furthermore, the author points out / stresses …. This becomes obvious in line … |
Besides, his father attaches great importance to … |
All in all, it becomes clear that the values the father believes in / holds onto …

FOCUS ON CHAPTER 2: THE TIES THAT BIND

9

Read the chapter. Then answer the questions below.

1. Why does Sarfraz's brother urinate out of his bedroom window?

2. Why was Navela not allowed to attend high school at first?

3. Why did Mohammed not let Navela pursue a career in fashion design?

4. What makes Sohail return from the USA to England?

5. Why does Mohammed feel let down by his children?

6. How does the family react to the mother's stroke?

7. How does the mother feel about her situation?

8. What is Uzma interested in and why?

9. How does Sohail react when Sarfraz suggests they make a documentary about the family?

Educating the children

10

a) **Pair work** One student collects information about Navela's education, the other about Sohail's education in the grid below. Then exchange the information.

Sohail	Navela

b) Contrast Mohammed's attitude towards his children's education. Use the language support from the box.

Language support

Comparing

When comparing / contrasting ... it is striking that ...
Unlike x, y seems to have a rather negative | uncompromising | conservative | critical | positive | favourable | attitude towards ...

In contrast to ...
Compared to x, y seems ...
whereas ... | however ... | similarly ... | whilst ... | on the other hand ... | likewise ...

c) Write a conversation Navela has with her best friend in which she reflects on her education and the opppurtunities she is given by her father.

d) **Group work (4)** Explain the attitudes of the friends of their parents towards education as portrayed in the following quote: "When I was a young boy I would hear my parents' friends advise them not to educate their children, because once they had an education they would no longer have anything to say." *(p. 83)*

Placemat Discuss their point of view in your group using the placemat method:
- Think about the advice individually.
- Write your ideas into your section of the placemat.
- Turn the placemat clockwise so that you can read your teammates' ideas.
- Discuss your ideas and agree on a result, which you write into the group section.
- Present your results in front of the class.

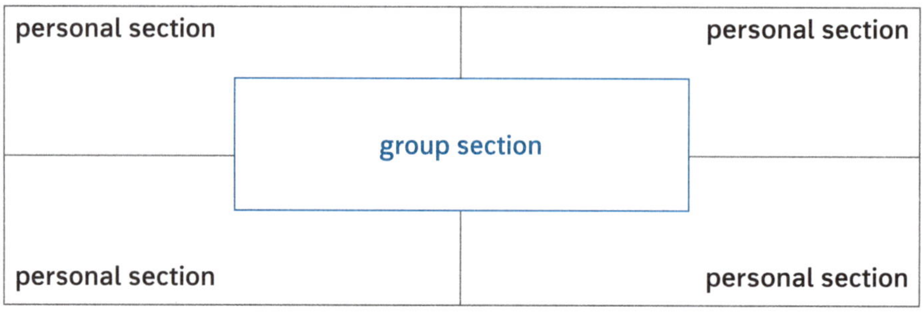

England's image

11

a) **Pair work** Revise the reasons why Mohammed Manzoor has come to England in the first place.

____

____

b) **Pair work** Interpret how the different people view England in the two extracts below. Partner A takes the first extract, partner B the second.

extract A	interpretation
I asked him what he made of life in Britain. He pulled a face as if chewing a piece of mango pickle. "Life is very hard," he complained. "People here work like dogs for their money." Bloody cheek, I thought to myself. There are millions desperate to come to England and now you're here, you're complaining. "Life is hard here but you do have the chance to have a better life than in Pakistan," I reminded him. He shook his head. "There is poverty in Pakistan, of course there is, but the rich live very well there. Servants, imported goods. A lifestyle you cannot imagine." I had thought that my brother-in-law would thank the stars we had taken him away from Pakistan, but instead he appeared to be in shock at the realisation that in Britain the good life required hard work. That was one of the problems with arranged marriages and importing husbands and wives from Pakistan: they thought marriage was a free ticket to an easy life. *(pp. 67-68)*	
extract B	**interpretation**
I have very few recollections from the trip. Each day was a flurry of meeting cousins and aunts and uncles. What I remember most clearly was a conversation where I was talking to some of my cousins and they were telling me how appalling England was. I sat sipping tea as they denounced England as being the home of sin and decadence and amorality. I could not be bothered to disagree or argue with them and so sat in silence. Finally they stopped talking. The room was quiet. "So tell me," piped up one of the cousins, a portly man with a large belly and full moustache, "could you help me get to England?" *(p. 72)*	

c) After these encounters Sarfraz sends Uzma text messages in which he reflects his attitude towards his brother-in-law and his cousins. Write his text messages. You may start like this:

And why's that?

Navela's husband still surprises me a lot.

A BBC programme

12

a) Collect information about the programme *Luton Actually* from the text.

____

____

____

____

b) Explain why Sohail is against taking part in the documentary.
c) Imagine you are Riete, the documentary director, talking to Sarfraz's family. Explain what the documentary is supposed to be about and outline some ideas of the documentary.
d) **Pair work** Discuss to what extent such documentaries help gain a better understanding among different ethnic groups.
e) OPTIONAL Choose an area in a city or town of your choice and make a 5-minute documentary about it focussing on the ethnic groups in your hometown.

FOCUS ON CHAPTER 3: BLOOD BROTHERS

13

Read the chapter. Complete the statements (1 to 8) by ticking (✓) the right answers (a, b, or c). Sometimes **more than one answer** is correct. Give evidence from the chapter.

1. When he is surrounded by Asians, Sarfraz feels ...
   - ☐ a) ... at ease.
   - ☒ b) ... out of place.
   - ☐ c) ... grateful.

   evidence: S. 89

2. His new friend Amolak ...
   - ☐ a) ... is confident.
   - ☒ b) ... is a Sikh.
   - ☐ c) ... is a Muslim.

   evidence: S. 89

3. Sarfraz thinks that ...
   - ☒ a) ... Bruce Springsteen is something for older people.
   - ☐ b) ... Amolak's taste of music is cool.
   - ☒ c) ... Bruce Springsteen does not care about his fans.

   evidence: S. 90

4. Sarfraz becomes ...
   - ☒ a) ... very enthusiastic about Springsteen.
   - ☐ b) ... annoyed by his music.
   - ☐ c) ... bored with his music.

   evidence: S. 91

5. When Sarfraz visits Amolak, his friend ...
- ☐ a) ... likes to talk to Mr Manzoor.
- ☐ b) ... welcomes Mr Manzoor.
- ☒ c) ... addresses his parents in Punjabi.

evidence: S. 95

6. After their first Springsteen concert, the boys feel ...
- ☐ a) ... absolutely thrilled.
- ☒ b) ... sad.
- ☐ c) ... happy.

evidence: ______

7. In later years the two friends ...
- ☒ a) ... attend as many concerts as they can.
- ☒ b) ... personally meet Bruce Springsteen.
- ☐ c) ... become friends of Springsteen's.

evidence: ______

8. The two friends have always ...
- ☐ a) ... had Asian girlfriends.
- ☒ b) ... been outsiders.
- ☒ c) ... favoured 'white' music.

evidence: ______

Friendship

14

a) **Group work (5)** Outline the history of Sarfraz's friendship with Amolak. Start with their encounter in the school cantine.

occasion	friendship
1. first encounters in school:	
2. the following weeks:	
3. Sunday evenings:	
4. the first Springsteen concert:	
5. from 1992-2006:	

b) Examine the portrayal of their relationship. Consider ...
- the words the author chooses to describe their relationship.
- the issues the author reports on.
- the reasons why this relationship is different from others.

c) **Think-Pair-Share**
Think Read the quotes about friendship. Choose the one that fits Sarfraz and Amolak's friendship best.
Pair Exchange your ideas with a partner.
Share Present your ideas in class.

1. Friendship ... is born at the moment when one man says to another "What! You too? I thought that no one but myself ..."
C.S. Lewis

2. Friendship is unnecessary, like philosophy, like art ... It has no survival value; rather it is one of those things which give value to survival.
C.S. Lewis

3. What is a friend? A single soul dwelling in two bodies. *Aristotle*

4. Each friend represents a world in us, a world possibly not born until they arrive, and it is only by this meeting that a new world is born. *Anais Nin*

Bruce Springsteen

15

a) Look at the quotes and explain how Springsteen's music influences Sarfraz and Amolak and contributes to their growing admiration or love for the musician.

quote	explanation
1. I [...] asked him what was on the cassette tapes. "Only the greatest music ever recorded, my friend," Amolak replied. "You woke up a boy and tonight you will go to sleep a man." *(p. 91)*	
2. The first thing that struck me was his voice; I had been expecting music and singing but Bruce Springsteen was not singing, he was just talking with an acoustic guitar playing in the background. "When I was growing up," he was saying, "me and my dad would go at it all the time, over almost anything." I was confused. This was not a song, it was a spoken word introduction to a song; it was a man recalling his childhood and his relationship with his father. *(p. 92)*	
3. Having stumbled in the dark for so long, on that September night I was blinded by the light. Everything significant that I did or achieved in my life in the years that followed had its roots in the emotions I experienced that evening. That night Bruce Springsteen changed my life. *(p. 93)*	
4. "The thing about Bruce," Amolak said, "is that it's like he knows everything you've ever felt, everything you've ever wanted and he can describe it better than you. [...] [T]here isn't a situation you will ever go through that Bruce will not have a song for." *(p. 96)*	
5. Springsteen had just finished singing 'Badlands' when he requested an acoustic guitar and told the audience: 'a fella came up to me and asked for this song. I don't know if he's out there tonight, but if he is, this is for you.' [...] I doubled up, buried my face in my hands and wept. [...] I never imagined I would hear it sung acoustically. The fact that Springsteen had remembered my request and then decided to actually listen to my suggestion was overwhelming. *(p. 116)*	

b) **Group work (4)** Have you ever shared a similar attitude towards a musician like the two young men have? If so, explain what musician, what kind of music and how. If not, explain whether you can understand such an attitude.

FOCUS ON CHAPTER 4: THE PROMISED LAND

16

Read the chapter. Then answer the questions below.

1. How do the Manzoors spend their holidays and why?

2. How does Sarfraz as a young boy view the USA?

3. What do Sarfraz's parents think about going to the cinema?

4. How does Sarfraz get to see American films?

5. How does his father react to the news that Sarfraz is going to the USA for a job?

6. On what occasions does Sarfraz travel to the United States?

First encounter

17

Describe how Sarfraz starts becoming fascinated by the USA.

American History

18

Sarfraz refers to some milestones in American history and some important politicians *(p. 130, ll. 20-28)*.

a) Match the photos to the events or people listed below.

1. John F. Kennedy ☐
2. Black Civil Rights Movement ☐
3. Freedom Riders ☐
4. Martin Luther King ☐
5. Rosa Parks ☐

a

b

c

d

e

b) **Group work (4-5)** Find out about the events and people on the Internet or in books. Collect 5-7 interesting pieces of information and share them with your group members.

aspects	notes
John F. Kennedy	
black Civil Rights Movement	
Rosa Parks	
Freedom Riders	
Martin Luther King	

c) Explain what role Martin Luther King and Malcolm X play for Sarfraz when he says: "In the absence of British Pakistani role models I borrowed Martin Luther King and Malcolm X." *(p. 130).*

d) **Pair work** Discuss the importance of political role models for young people now and then. In your discussion consider the following questions:
- Are there any political role models you know or have got?
- How important is it for young people to have such role models?
- Do politicians have to set moral as well as political standards?

Views on the USA

19

a) **Group work (4-5)** Read the extracts below and analyse Sarfraz's view on and interest in the USA.

extracts	analysis
1. I had been fascinated with the United States for as long as I could remember; for me it was a magical crucible from which spewed fantastic films and marvellous music. *(p. 124)*	
2. Although I had always fancied America, after Mary's slide show I fell headlong in love with the country. On Saturdays when Navela would take me to Luton Central Library I would take out travel guides to New York and California and construct imaginary itineraries that traversed the length and breadth of the nation. *(p. 125)*	
3. I followed the American elections almost as avidly as the British ones and even compiled my own cuttings file on the 1984 Presidential campaign. When family and friends came to visit my father would call me downstairs and ask me to tell the guests who the American President was. *(p. 125)*	
4. The more bored I was with my life in Luton the more America appealed. All my hopes were encapsulated in the life I imagined was possible in the United States. *(p. 130)*	

extracts	analysis
5. For all my interest in the black struggle I was not black, I had not read of any discrimination against Pakistanis in America and so the United States remained a place for second chances. *(pp. 130-131)*	
6. I kept returning to the United States. In my final year at university I took out a student loan and used it to fly to Los Angeles for two weeks. I dared not tell my family I had done anything quite so reckless; they suspected nothing although the next time I returned to Luton they did ask me how it was that I had developed such a deep suntan in the middle of January. *(p. 151)*	
7. Once I started working I thought nothing of flying to the United States three or four times a year. I would take off on my own and spend a week in Seattle, a long weekend in New York City, traverse the country by Amtrak to see America by rail. Each time Bruce Springsteen toured it was another excuse to go; I saw him in Pittsburgh on one tour and New Jersey, New York and Washington on another. *(p. 151)*	
8. With each visit the less special travelling to the United States became; going to the country I had fantasised about for so long had become almost routine. It was never as viscerally thrilling, never as filled with wonderment and awe as it was during that first summer back when I was still a teenager. *(p. 151)*	

b) Describe Sarfraz's attitude towards the United States using your notes from the previous task.

Tip For his father's attitude study pages 125-126 and 134-135.

c) Compare Sarfraz and his father's attitude towards the USA.

→ **Language support** Comparing, p. 16

d) CHALLENGE Imagine you are Mohammed Manzoor: Write his interior monologue in which you explain his initial attitude towards the USA and his finally accepting Sarfraz's decision to go abroad.
You may start like this:
Sarfraz always surprises me, more than any other child of mine. First the letters from America ... Now he talks about ... What about the values ...?

FOCUS ON CHAPTER 5: FACTORY

20

Read the chapter. Match the sentence halves.

1. Mohammed spends his working years on a production line
2. Pakistani parents, who work hard for their living,
3. Sarfraz lets down his parents
4. When Sarfraz has a job
5. Sarfraz has to hand over all the money he earns
6. The money the family members earn
7. Sohail helps his brother
8. His father saves money for his retirement
9. Sarfraz lands his first real job
10. In his speech at the reopening of his former school,

a) to pay his rent.
b) on the day of Bruce Springsteen's birthday.
c) to travel to Mecca and India.
d) Sarfraz encourages the pupils to work hard for their dreams.
e) is often sent to relatives in Pakistan.
f) to his parents.
g) to make sure his family has enough to eat.
h) when his results are weaker than those of Tanveer's.
i) want their children to do better in life.
j) his parents treat him like a grown-up.

1	2	3	4	5	6	7	8	9	10

Parents

21

a) Describe how Tanveer's parents push their son to excel in anything he does.

____

____

b) Illustrate the work ethic Asian parents have according to the author.

c) **Pair work** Analyse Sarfraz's parents' attitude towards Sarfraz's achievements in the extracts below.

extracts	analysis
1. My parents had seemed reasonably satisfied and I had retired to bed feeling mightily relieved. *(p. 156)*	
2. I told him Tanveer's results. It was not just my father who exploded with rage, my mother was also livid. 'So this is how you thank us,' screamed my father, 'making us look like fools in front of his mother and father? Do you know how hard they must be laughing at us in their house?' *(p. 157)*	

extracts	analysis
3. Tanveer's better grades meant that I had committed the worst of crimes: I had embarrassed my parents in front of others. I had let them down. *(p. 157)*	
4. In the end, the only thing parents want from their children is for them to do them proud. I knew my mother was proud but it was impossible not to think about the man who was not there to see the journey reach full circle. I know it would have made my father hugely proud to have seen me open my old school [...] *(p. 177)*	

Sarfraz's jobs

22

a) List the jobs Sarfraz had until he became a full-time journalist.

____

b) Examine the attitude Sarfraz shows towards these jobs.

c) **Group work** CHOOSE Talk about your own job experience in your group: Have you got a part-time or weekend job? What do you do? Explain why or why not?

OR

When Sarfraz is already a well-known author, he is asked to hold a speech at the reopening of his former school. In his speech he says: "You can do anything you want in this world [...] You just need to work hard and dare to want more from life." *(p. 176)*

Explain his advice. Discuss if you agree with his message.

Earning money

23

a) Describe Mr Manzoor's attitude towards making money according to the author.

____

____

b) Compare Sarfraz and his father's attitude towards making money.

→ **Language support** Comparing, p. 16

c) **Pair work** Rank your own attitude towards making money according to a scale ranging from 1 (saving money) to 6 (spending money) and explain your decision to a partner.

The charity race

24

a) Find out …

1. … the name of the charity race.	
2. … the organizer's name.	
3. … how much Sarfraz trains.	
4. … who Sarfraz asks to sponsor him.	
5. … how the race goes.	
6. … how much money Sarfraz collects.	
7. … who should profit from the charity money.	
8. … what Sarfraz does in fact with the money.	

b) **Group work (3)** Good angel versus bad angel
Write a discussion as Sarfraz's conscience.

- First collect arguments and reasons in your group why Sarfraz should keep the sponsoring money or donate the money.
- Then have one student as Sarfraz sit on a chair with the other two students as angels standing behind him and representing his conscience.
- Act out the concience conversation / discussion. At the end of their conversation, Sarfraz has to decide which side he finds more convincing.

You may start like this:
Sarfraz: "What if I keep the money instead of donating it? It's so tempting to keep the money! …"

Language support

Challenging your opponent's arguments
Are you sure? / As I see it, …
I would like to remind you that …
It just isn't true that …
The point / problem is …
There's simply no proof that …
It may be true that …, but …
You're quite wrong there
I'm sorry, but I don't agree at all
That's an exaggeration because …

FOCUS ON CHAPTER 6: BETTER DAYS

25

Read the chapter. Then complete the sentences. Tick the correct box. There may be **more than one** correct answer.

1. Sarfraz never …
- ❑ sees his parents touch each other.
- ❑ hears his parents talk about their wedding day.
- ❑ hears his parents address each other by their first names.
- ❑ sees his parents argue with each other.

2. On weekends …
- ❑ the Manzoors often visit friends.
- ❑ the family watches Bollywood films.
- ❑ the family goes on outings.
- ❑ the Manzoors watch Indian films with their friends.

3. When Sarfraz is small ...
   - ❑ his father teaches him to read the Koran.
   - ❑ he is afraid that he might be punished in Hell.
   - ❑ he is afraid of seeing characters on TV kiss each other.
   - ❑ he enjoys watching TV with his family.

4. As a teenager Sarfraz ...
   - ❑ goes out with some girls.
   - ❑ fancies some girls at school.
   - ❑ imagines a girlfriend.
   - ❑ is good at school.

5. For Sarfraz's father love ...
   - ❑ is a feeling that weakens a person's rational behaviour.
   - ❑ is overpowering.
   - ❑ is a feeling for the naive.
   - ❑ is important.

6. At a Pakistani wedding ...
   - ❑ the couple looks happy.
   - ❑ the bride wears a lot of jewellery.
   - ❑ Sarfraz realizes that he, too, will be married off to a stranger one day.
   - ❑ Sarfraz realizes that it is important to have a family.

7. When he works at a factory, Sarfraz ...
   - ❑ meets a nice white girl he falls in love with.
   - ❑ asks a Pakistani girl to watch a film with him.
   - ❑ tells the girl's father about his invitation.
   - ❑ makes a Pakistani girl realize how much she enjoys being with him.

8. In order to find a suitable partner,
   - ❑ Sarfraz wants to visit a village in Pakistan.
   - ❑ Sarfraz goes speed-dating.
   - ❑ Sarfraz wants to meet the girls' parents.
   - ❑ Sarfraz's mother arranges some dates for her son.

Finding a partner

26 Group work (3)

a) Talk to your group members about the following questions and take some notes:
- What are your plans for the future?
- Do you want to get married one day? Why, why not?
- How much do you listen to your parents' advice when you choose a partner?
- What do you consider to be a more important aspect in a relationship: love or sense?

____

____

____

____

b) Look at the following excerpts and analyse the character's attitude towards love and marriage: Choose adjectives that best describe their attitude from the box below and explain your choice. The first one has been done for you in the table on the right.

annoyed | awkward | clever | conservative | disappointed | embarrased | far-sighted | frustrated | indifferent | intelligent | irritated | logical | matter-of-fact | mature | narrow-minded | old-fashioned | rational | realistic | sensible | traditional | wise

Language support

When it comes to ... he / she seems ...
This can be seen ... when he / she ...
Furthermore, he / she sounds rather ..., which becomes clear when ....
His / Her attitude can be described as ...
This excerpt shows how ...

extracts	analysis
Sarfraz's parents	
1. If two characters were kissing we would all at first pretend it was not happening, [...] my father would spontaneously start a conversation. The longer and more intense the kiss, the more discomforting it was for my family; my father would start grumbling and my mother would be murmuring about how whites were lacking in all shame. *(p. 184)*	*father: feels embarrassed and awkward when witnessing intimate situations on TV; mother thinks kissing is too intimate a situation to be shared and shown on TV → love is a feeling you do not show in public*
2. My father treated the concept of love with a withering mixture of contempt and pity. 'What is love, anyway?' he would ask. 'Love is childish, anyone can fall in love, a ten-year-old can say they are in love but can you trust a ten-year-old to stay with the same person for forty years?' *(p. 187)*	
3. 'Being happy?' retorted my father. 'You think that's what marriage is about? Marriage is about commitment and family and having someone to look after you when you get old.' *(p. 189)*	

extracts	analysis
Sarfraz	
4. When I was growing up I assumed that was what all marriages were like: arrangements, businesslike affairs. Love had very little to do with any of it. *(p. 179)*	
5. I knew my parents expected me to have an arranged marriage and anyway none of the girls at school fancied me. This was one of the cruellest consequences of being an Asian at a predominantly white school. *(p. 185)*	
6. Falling in love would have been deeply inconvenient as it would have involved my parents disowning me and throwing me out of their home. *(p. 186)*	

extracts	analysis
7. I didn't know what love felt like but according to the songs I was listening to when I was fourteen, it was overpowering and its power overwhelming. *(p. 186)*	
8. When you fell in love it seemed you no longer had control over your emotions and you became a slave to your desires. This scared me. *(p. 187)*	

extracts	analysis
Navela	
9. Navela had spent the first ten years of her life in Pakistan but it still shocked me that she was so unconcerned about marrying somebody she didn't know. 'Just so long as he's not shorter than me,' was her main stipulation. *(p. 194)*	
10. After my father died Navela came to our home and urged my mother to marry off both me and my sister. We hardly saw her, but she felt it was her duty as the eldest to set us straight. *(p. 199)*	
11. Navela looked blankly back at me. I had hoped my sister and brother would have a more enlightened view, they seemed loath to offer me the freedom they had not enjoyed. *(p. 199)*	

c) Compare your understanding of finding a partner with that of the Manzoors.

→ **Language support** Comparing, p. 16

Nazia

27

a) Collect information about Nazia in the grid below.

aspects	
clothes:	**language:**
marriage:	**job / way of living:**

b) Explain how Nazia differs from Sarfraz's understanding of a Pakistani woman. Use the information collected in task a).

FOCUS ON CHAPTER 7: REASON TO BELIEVE

28

a) Scan the chapter. Then complete the sentences below in one to five words. There is an example at the beginning (0).

Christmas

0 At Christmas the shops run by Pakistanis *stay open*.

1. At Christmas Mr Manzoor works ______________________________

2. Mrs Manzoor comforts Sarfraz and his little sister when they are shocked about Jesus' murder by

____

3. The week before Christmas the pupils bring toys into the school but Sarfraz ______________________________

____

Reading the Koran

4. There are a lot of rules about reading the Koran such as ______________________________

____

5. Sarfraz's mother teaches her children Arabic by ______________________________

____

6. Sarfraz and his sister learn Arabic and Urdu simultaneously as ______________________________

____

7. Before Sarfraz reads the Koran in the evening, he ______________________________

____

8. The pupils at school ask Sarfraz ______________________________

____

Eid (a major Islamic festival)

9. Sarfraz loves Eid for ______________________________

____

10. Sarfraz does not enjoy visiting the mosque for Eid because ______________________________

____

11. On Eid Sarfraz's friends from school come to his house to ______________________________

____

Fasting

12. Muslims fast to ______________________________

13. At Ramadan Sarfraz feels ______________________________

____

14. Mr Manzoor does not fast because ______________________________

____

Being a Muslim after 9/11

15. When the airplanes hit the Towers, Sarfraz is ______________________________

____

16. 9/11 changes Sarfraz's life in so far as ______________________________

____

17. When Sarfraz is asked about the purpose of his stay, he tells the immigration officers at JFK ______________________________

____

Being a Muslim

29

a) **Think-Pair-Share**
Think List what Sarfraz seems to think makes a good Muslim.
Pair Compare your list with your partner.
Share Present your findings in class.

____

____

____

b) **Pair work** Analyse the role religion plays for Sarfraz when he is growing up: Mark the importance of religion for him on the line below and explain your decision. Give evidence from the text to prove your point.

religion

important ←——————————————→ **unimportant**

c) Explain what Sarfraz means when he says: "It was only many years later that I realised it was not Islam I was reacting against, it was the cultural values of my parents' generation." *(p. 227)*

9/11

30

a) Use the webcode and find out about ... **Webcode** **DSW-73685-04**
- what happened on 9/11/2001.
- how it happened.
- who was held responsible for it.
- what happened in the aftermath.

b) **Pair work** Exchange your information with a partner.
c) Explain how 9/11 changes Sarfraz's life in the following excerpts.

extracts	explanation
1. For the first thirty years of my life I had been running away from my religion but on 9/11 my religion caught up with me. There was nowhere left to hide. *(p. 235)*	

extracts	explanation
2. "Me and you, Sarfraz, we always thought, fuck this country; if Britain does not want us we always have America. Not anymore, mate, now we are going to have to do what we can in this here country because you know that the second you try to land at JFK they are going to haul your arse into jail. [...]" *(p. 235)*	
3. Earlier that summer there had been rioting in three British towns. At the time the disturbances in Bradford, Burnley and Oldham had been described as 'race riots' between Asian or Pakistani youths and the police. After 9/11 it was no longer about Pakistanis, Indians and Bengalis but Muslims, Hindus and Sikhs. *(p. 236)*	
4. I dreaded to think what arriving in JFK might be like following the attacks; the newspaper reports of innocent Asians being detained for questioning and then slung back to Britain confirmed Amolak's grim theory that the United States was no longer our promised land. I cancelled my flight. It took a few days for me to notice the irony: I was scared of flying because I was scared that others would be scared of me not because I was frightened of terrorism. *(p. 236)*	

At immigration

31

a) Briefly describe the atmosphere at JFK airport.
Use the adjectives below and give evidence from the text.

charged | emotional | gloomy | heady | highly friendly | homely | hostile | relaxed | tense

Language support

Describing the atmosphere

The atmosphere can be described as ......
This becomes obvious on page ... when ...
It is further characterized as ..., which is apparent when ...
It seems ... Evidence can be found on page ... when ...

At JFK airport

b) **Pair work** One partner steps into Sarfraz's shoes. The other one steps into the immigration officer's shoes.

Sarfraz: Imagine you are Sarfraz queueing up for passport control. Jot down what is going on in your mind by answering the following questions:
- How are you feeling?
- What are you afraid of?
- What are you thinking?
- What are you hoping?

Immigration officer: Imagine you are an immigration officer checking the passports at JFK after 9/11. You are on full alert. Jot down what is going on in your mind by answering the following questions:
- How are you feeling about arriving passengers?
- What are you afraid of?
- What are you thinking when you see Sarfraz Manzoor?
- What are you thinking when you hear that he has come to see Bruce Springsteen?

c) **Group work (4)**
- Present your ideas to another pair.
- Then decide on a final version and act out the scene: Two students take Sarfraz's part, the other two take the immigration officer's part. While Sarfraz and the immigration officer mime their action silently, the other two students stand behind their characters and speak their minds.

d) Write a blog post and discuss how music in general, and Bruce Springsteen in particular, can contribute to a better understanding among people. → **S7** Checklist: writing a block post

FOCUS ON CHAPTER 8: LAND OF HOPE AND DREAMS

32

Scan the chapter. Look at the captions and put them into the correct order. Give evidence from the text. The first one has been done for you.

captions	order	evidence
a) Terror attacks		
b) Now and then		
c) Feeling patriotic		
d) Made in England		
e) Being bullied		
f) Torn between England and Pakistan	1.	*pp. 240-246*
g) Visiting Pakistan		
h) Britain's changing		

Visiting Pakistan

33

a) **Group work (4)** Describe the pictures and talk about your impressions of Pakistan.

b) **Group work (4)** Study pages 245-251. Outline how the family members seem to feel about their visit to Pakistan.

Mrs Manzoor:	
Mr Manzoor:	
Sarfraz:	
his siblings:	

c) Explain what Sarfraz says about his father:

"In some ways my father was more English than he was Pakistani. He was like an Asian reincarnation of a traditional Victorian father: emotionally repressed; a strong belief in discipline and authority; faith in the value of hard work and education, and a disdain for excessive emoting." *(p. 251)*

d) Contrast the differing attitudes towards their stay in Pakistan using the notes from the previous task.

→ **Language support** Comparing p. 16

e) CHOOSE

Imagine you are Sarfraz's mother. Write a letter to her family in which she reflects upon her stay in Pakistan.

OR

Imagine you are Sarfraz's father. Write his interior monologue in which he reflects upon his stay in Pakistan.

→ **Workshop** Writing an interior monologue

Enoch Powell

34

Not all English people welcomed immigrants from the former colonies. British MP Enoch Powell gave a speech in which he strongly criticized mass immigration, especially immigration from the former colonies. His speech held on 20 April 1968 is known as the "Rivers of Blood"-speech.

Enoch Powell, 1912-1998

a) Read extracts from the speech.

	Summary
It almost passes belief that at this moment 20 or 30 additional immigrant children are arriving from overseas in Wolverhampton[1] alone every week – and that means 15 or 20 additional families a decade or two hence. Those whom the gods wish to destroy, they first make mad[2]. We must be mad, literally mad, as a nation to be permitting the annual inflow[3] of some 50,000 dependents[4], who are for the most part the material of the future growth of the immigrant descended population. It is like watching a nation busily engaged in heaping up[5] its own funeral pyre[6]. So insane are we that we actually permit unmarried persons to immigrate for the purpose of founding a family with spouses[7] and fiancées[8] whom they have never seen. [...]	
In these circumstances nothing will suffice[9] but that the total inflow for settlement should be reduced at once to negligible[10] proportions, and that the necessary legislative and administrative measures be taken without delay. I stress the words "for settlement." This has nothing to do with the entry of Commonwealth citizens, any more than of aliens[11], into this country, for the purposes of study or of improving their qualifications, like (for instance)[12] the Commonwealth doctors who, to the advantage of their own countries, have enabled our hospital service to be expanded faster than would otherwise have been possible. They are not, and never have been, immigrants. [...]	
As I look ahead, I am filled with foreboding[13]. Like the Roman, I seem to see "the river Tiber foaming with much blood"[14]. [...] All I know is that to see, and not to speak, would be the great betrayal.	

Annotations

1 **Wolverhampton** = E. Powell was MP for a Wolverhampton constituency
2 **Those whom ... mad** = Roman saying attributed to Publius Syrus
3 **annual inflow** = the arrival [of people] every year
4 **dependent** = a person who depends on the state for a home, food or money
5 to **heap up sth** = *etw. aufhäufen*
6 **funeral pyre** = *Scheiterhaufen*
7 **spouse** = a husband or a wife
8 **fiancée** = the woman a man is engaged to
9 **suffice** = to be enough for sth
10 **negligible** = insignificant
11 **alien** = a person who is not a citizen of the country they live in
12 **for instance** = for example
13 **foreboding** = a feeling that sth unpleasant or dangerous is going to happen
14 **to see "The river Tiber foaming with much blood"** = In his prophesy to his son Aeneas, the mythological forefather of the Romans, Anchises, lays out the future to his son: before the Roman Empire will be finally established a lot of wars need to be fought on Italian soil. Whereas Anchises implies that a lot of suffering (wars) is needed until world power is finally reached, Powell misuses the quote to predict that mass immigration might lead to either a high crime rate or civil unrest.

b) Sum up each extract with one sentence.
c) **Pair work** Explain ...
- the meaning of the Roman saying: "Those whom the gods wish to destroy, they first make mad."
- what "sort of immigrants" Powell warns against.
- what measures Powell suggests.
- what sort of people Powell welcomes.

d) CHALLENGE Analyse the language Powell uses to show his point of view.
e) Watch the youtube video. Then answer the questions below and takes notes. You can find a link to the video here: **Webcode** **DSW-73685-05**

	Notes		
1. What did E. Powell do before he gave the speech?			
2. How did the Shadow Cabinet Powell belonged to react to his speech?			
3. How did people on the street react to the speech?			
4. How did Paul Uppdal's parents feel about the speech?			
5. How much has become reality of what Powell predicted according to Paul Uppdal?			
6. How does Bill Etheridge assess Powell's speech?			
7. What have immigrants contributed to according to Ian Austin? Tick the fields that are mentioned.	❑ community life ❑ economy ❑ businesses	❑ communal spirit ❑ multiculturalism ❑ politics	❑ international food ❑ cultural diversity ❑ jobs

f) Read the following passage in the book: page 254, ll. 12-25. Explain how Enoch Powell and other politicians have influenced the Manzoors' way of living.

7/7/2005

35

a) Find out about the 7/7/2005 bombings: Do some research on the Internet. Then put the phrases below into the correct order and form sentences with them.

victims | (to) detonate bombs | British-born sons of Pakistani immigrants | on London Underground trains | (to) be packed in backpacks | on a double-decker bus | (to) carry out suicide attacks

___

___

___

b) Describe how Sarfraz feels about the bombings and the people behind the attacks.

c) **CHALLENGE** Imagine Sarfraz writes a letter to the editor in which he expresses his thoughts and feelings about the suicide bombers and their motifs. Write his letter. → **S4** Checklist: Letter to the editor

Home

36

a) **Pair work** What is home to you? Where do you feel you belong to? Do you feel accepted by society? Discuss these questions with a partner.

b) **Group work (5)** Read the following passages and examine Sarfraz's attitude towards Britain: Find out how he feels about Britain and what factors influence his attitude.

Luton

1. p. 255, ll. 18-29
2. p. 256, ll. 14-25
3. p. 258, ll. 9-15
4. p. 260, l. 24 to p. 261, l. 17
5. p. 269, ll. 4-13

FOCUS ON THE AFTERWORD: THE PROMISE

37

a) Read the chapter. Then decide which summary fits best. Explain your choice.
   1. In his afterword Manzoor explains how he met his wife and how Bruce Springsteen's music made him take the steps he then took and why he wrote the book in the first place.
   2. The afterword is about Manzoor looking back at the life he led as a teenager and the life he now lives with his wife and children.
   3. The afterword is about Manzoor tackling the problems he had to face as a teenager and adult and living up to his dreams that were inspired by Bruce Springsteen's songs.

b) Explain what Manzoor means when he says: "The prospect of a life where I had a job I hated or only tolerated felt a betrayal of that promise as did the prospect of spending my life with someone who I did not, in the words from 'Born to Run,' love with 'all the madness in my soul.'" *(p. 273)*

1. Name two things that are changing for Muslims in the UK.	*a)* *b)*
2. In which two fields can changes be seen?	*a)* *b)*
3. What can young Muslims aim for nowadays?	
4. Name two posts that are held by British Asians.	*a)* *b)*
5. What does Manzoor think about these changes?	

c) Discuss if you agree with Manzoor's attitude towards life.

Changes for British Muslims in the UK

38

a) Listen to Sarfraz Manzoor talking about the changes for Muslims in the UK and fill in the table. You can find a link to the video here: **Webcode** DSW-73685-06

b) Having come across the blog "Successful British Asians in the UK – Myth or Reality?" you have decided to leave a guest post assessing whether British Asians can be successful in the UK today. Write this blog post using the information from the interview. → **S7** Checklist: Writing a blog post

POST-READING

LOOKING BACK AT THE NOVEL

At the end of this unit you are going to create your own film version of the book and pitch your idea to a production company. In preparation for this task complete the following exercises.

The Manzoors and their friends

39

a) **Group work** Make a poster about one of the major characters, using the information you have collected in the course of the reading. In your group decide what information should be included.

b) Present your posters to the class in a Gallery walk.

Major scenes or events

40 Group work (3-4)

a) Decide on the most important scenes or events described in the book. Use a symbol to indicate what the scene is about, headline the scene and summarize it in one sentence. The first scene has been done for you.

b) Then present your ideas to the class.

Scene 1	*Scene 2*	...

Arrival in England *Sarfraz arrives in England with his mother and siblings to join his father.*		

Relevance of the songs by Bruce Springsteen

41 Group work

a) In the pre-reading section, you talked about the songs that Sarfraz uses as headings for his chapters. Get together in your (old) groups and examine how the songs' contents relate to the chapters from the memoir. Use your reading journal for help.

b) Present your findings to the class.

c) Form new expert groups and discuss the importance of Bruce Springsteen and his songs for the author.

→ **Language support** Challenging your opponent's arguments, p. 27

Memoirs

42

a) Read the info box below and find out why *Greetings from Bury Park* is classified as a memoir. Use your reading journal for help.

Info

A memoir is a nonfictional narrative based on the author's personal experiences. One of the earliest and most famous memoirs is Julius Caesar's *Commentaries on the Gallic Wars*, better known as *De Bello Gallico*, in which he describes the battles and the intrigues that took place between 58 and 49 BC.
Up until the 20th century memoirs were usually written by famous politicians, military leaders or people in court[1] society who had achieved something great and unusual and who were skilled writers. Since cheap digital book productions at the turn of the 21st century there has been an immense increase in this genre.
Whereas an autobiography looks back on the author's life in a chronological narrative, memoirs usually focus on particular events in an author's social life and explore issues that have played an important role in the author's past and have shaped his or her identity. Memoirs help the author come to terms with past events and pass down his or her personal legacies[2], thus functioning as therapy.

[1] **court** = *höfisch*
[2] **legacy** = here: tradition, experience

b) **Pair work** Identify elements of a memoir in *Greetings from Bury Park*.

____

____

c) Speculate about the reasons why Sarfraz Manzoor has chosen this genre.

A modern version

43

Imagine you are a director and are asked to turn Sarfraz Manzoor's *Greetings from Bury Park* into a modern film version. Design this version.

1. Original title: ***Greetings from Bury Park***
2. Title of the film version?
3. Genre? Will it be a coming-of-age film? A mockumentary? A comedy? A teen drama? Another genre?
4. Setting: What settings do you choose?
5. Casting of actors: What are the main roles? What actors and actresses are going to play them?

A pitch

44

a) **Pair work** Prepare the pitch, in which you ...
- summarize the original book.
- present your reason for making such a film.
- talk about the relevance of the book for our society.
- outline the idea for your film version.

b) Present your ideas to the class. The other students function as the board of film producers and the production company. At the end of the presentations vote for the best presentation.

Info

A pitch

A pitch is a short oral presentation of an idea for a film or TV series, made by a director or script writer to convince a film producer to fund the project. As time is money, the presentation must be short and to the point.

CHALLENGE

45

Present elements of the memoir in the film version of *Greetings from Bury Park* called *Blinded by the light*.

BRITISHNESS

1

a) **Think-Pair-Share** What does Britishness mean to you?
Think Make a list with as many aspects that you can think of.
Pair Compare your list with a partner. Add any new ideas.
Share Share your ideas in class.

b) Watch the video and tick (✓) the things the people interviewed mention. You can find a link to the video here: **Webcode** DSW-73685-07

- ❑ 1. strong people
- ❑ 2. union of independent countries
- ❑ 3. different languages
- ❑ 4. collected identity
- ❑ 5. individualism
- ❑ 6. accepting other people
- ❑ 7. queuing up
- ❑ 8. being polite to other people
- ❑ 9. showing respect towards others
- ❑ 10. multiculturalism
- ❑ 11. variety of food
- ❑ 12. the Queen
- ❑ 13. Buckingham Palace
- ❑ 14. London Eye
- ❑ 15. walking the dog
- ❑ 16. having a cup of tea
- ❑ 17. intelligent people
- ❑ 18. lack of discrimination
- ❑ 19. William Shakespeare
- ❑ 20. colonialism
- ❑ 21. immigration
- ❑ 22. class
- ❑ 23. fish and chips
- ❑ 24. understanding irony

c) Group the aspects mentioned in the video and the ones you have listed in task a) to the categories below. Add new ones when necessary.

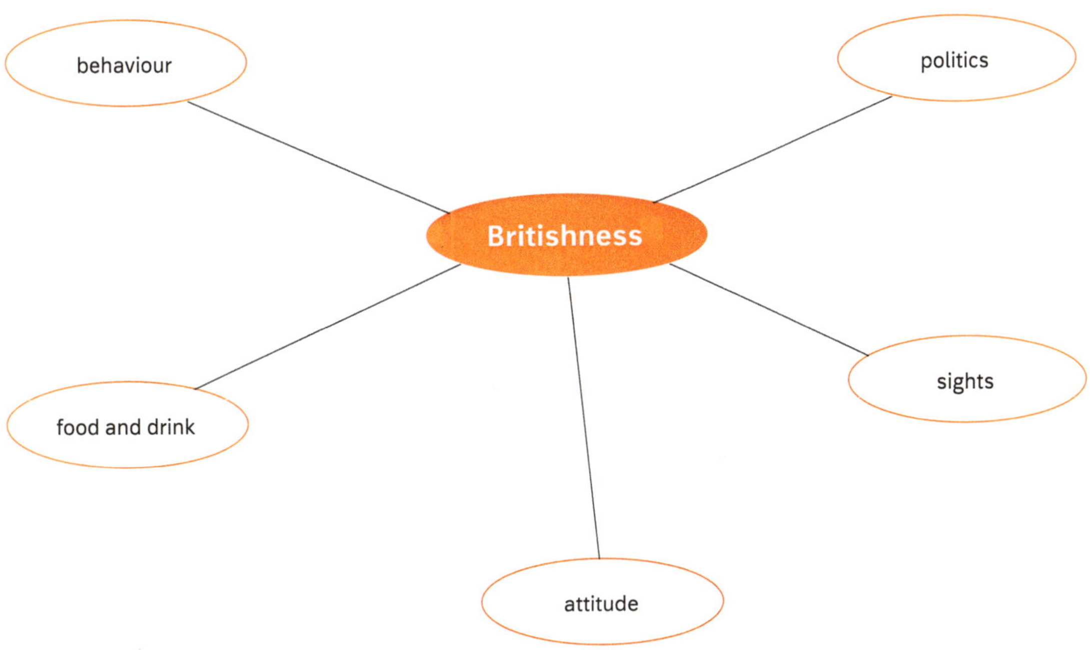

d) OPTIONAL Discuss what things define Germanness using the categories from task b).

MULTICULTURAL BRITAIN

2

a) Read the article published and updated on 5 September 2019 by *Great British Mag*, a digital magazine, that helps students abroad to gain insight into the British way of life.

Is the UK multicultural?

5 September 2019

The UK is most definitely multicultural, and it has always been. For a start, it's made up of four different nations. England, Scotland, Wales, and Northern Ireland are all different countries with different dialects, customs, music, and languages. [...]

The UK's colonial past also explains our multiculturalism. During the British Empire, many Britons went to live and work in colonies around the world and many colonial subjects[1] came to Britain. Even today, former territories and colonies have strong ties to Britain and people continue to migrate. Interestingly, the 2011 census revealed that the overall percentage of Brits who identify as white and Christian is declining. A separate study shows that over 300 languages are spoken in the UK.

However, this diversity is not evenly[2] spread across the UK. Big cities like London, Manchester, and Birmingham are extremely multicultural, but smaller towns and villages are far less so. This is because immigrants have historically flocked[3] to the larger cities in search of work.

Different cities in the UK also have different proportions of various ethnic groups depending on their individual histories. For example, Liverpool has an old black community because Liverpool was once linked to the trans-Atlantic slave trade. Liverpool is also home to the oldest Chinese community in Europe because of the city's strong trading ties with Shanghai dating back to the 1890s.

In recent years, there has been a noticeable increase in nationalistic sentiment in the UK because some Britons believe that the UK should not be multicultural. But many more Britons believe that our history shows us we have always been multicultural and that there are many economic and social benefits of being a multicultural nation.

If you have a question for our resident Brit drop us an email at askabrit@greatbritishmag.co.uk.

Annotations
[1] **subject** = a person who belongs to a particular country
[2] **evenly** = in a smooth and regular way
[3] (to) **flock to** = (to) move somewhere in large numbers

b) Outline the reasons why the UK is considered multicultural according to the article.

Britishness and multicultural Britain in the memoir

3

a) **Group work** Read the extracts and outline the main idea in one or two sentences.

extracts	outline	notes
1. *p. 221, ll. 18-30*		
2. *p. 251, ll. 9-16*		
3. *p. 254, ll. 12-25*		

extracts	outline	notes
4. *p. 264, ll. 4-21*		
5. *p. 267, l. 8 to p. 268, l. 11*		

b) Examine how Britishness and multicultural Britain are presented in the extracts. Use the notes section in the grid above.

c) CHALLENGE Use your notes from the previous task and write an article about the portrayal of multicultural Britain in *Greetings from Bury Park*: Don't forget a captivating headline.

→ **S8** How to improve your text

A discussion on the integration of ethnic minorities

4

You are going to carry out a discussion in class on the topic: How can integration be successful? In preparation for the discussion carry out the following tasks.

a) Pair work Roy Jenkins was Home Secretary from 1965-7 and a member of the Labour Party. Read and explain his view on integration expressed in 1966:

> "I do not regard [integration] as meaning the loss, by immigrants, of their own national characteristics and culture. I do not think that we need in this country a 'melting pot', which will turn everybody out in a common mould[1], as one of a series of carbon copies of someone's misplaced vision of the stereotyped Englishman... I define integration, therefore, not as a flattening process of assimilation but as equal opportunity, accompanied by cultural diversity, in an atmosphere of mutual tolerance."

[1] **mould** = frame

Group work (4)

b) Collect ideas about how integration can be successful in the following fields:
- community life (e.g. community centre, youth clubs, festivals etc.)
- school life (extracurricular activities, clubs, programmes etc.)
- politics (e.g. party members, policies etc.)
- cultural life (sports clubs, theatre, open mosque, church days etc.)

____

____

____

c) Choose 1-2 student(s) to host the discussion. They should collect questions for the participants. Each group chooses two members to take part in the discussion.

d) The host starts the discussion by welcoming the guests and by introducing the topic. At the end the host summarizes the ideas and draws a conclusion. → **S22** How to stage a debate

Who am I? (Ethnic) identity

5

a) Pair work Have you ever asked yourself who you are? What defines a person? What makes each of us who we are? Discuss this issue with your partner. Consider the following guiding questions:
- How much do the following factors shape your identity: gender, nationality, peer group, religion, outer appearance, traditions, family, hobbies and interests?
- What factors do you choose for yourself?
- What factors are determined for you by other people or by society?
- What role do feelings, empathy and sympathy play in forming one's identity?

b) Start a mind map about identity and complete it in the course of this theme. Note down ideas, aspects, vocabulary etc.

The concept of identity

6

Read the quotations about identity.

1. "So, I guess we are who we are for a lot of reasons. And maybe we'll never know most of them. But even if we don't have the power to choose where we come from, we can still choose where we go from there. We can still do things." (*Stephen Chbosky*)

2. "A rose by any other name would smell as sweet." (*William Shakespeare*)

3. "Every man is the architect of his own fortune." (*Appius*)

4. "Nothing of me is original. I am the combined effort of everyone I've ever known." (*Chuck Palahniuk*)

5. "Unlike a drop of water which loses its identity when it joins the ocean, man does not lose his being in the society in which he lives. Man's life is independent. He is born not for the development of the society alone, but for the development of his self." (*B.R. Ambedkar*)

a) Choose the one you like best and state why.
b) Explain how identity is presented in the quote.

The concept of ethnic identity

7

a) Read the info box about ethnic identity.
b) **Pair work** Then test your partner by asking him or her questions about the text.

Info

Ethnic identity

The term ethnic identity is a rather complex and multidimensional concept that has been researched in various disciplines such as psychology, sociology and anthropology. Although researchers cannot agree on a clear definition as to what aspects include a person's ethnic identity, there are four common elements:

1. **self-identification:** An individual sees themself as a member of an ethnic group.
2. **affective components:** An individual feels that he or she belongs to a certain group and shows certain behaviours and practices that are typical of this ethnic group.
3. **cognitive components:** A person has knowledge of the traditions, customs and the history of the ethnic group.
4. **value orientation:** A person holds cultural values associated with the ethnic group.

Ethnic identity can also be described as a measurement of how much people feel they belong to a certain cultural or social group This approach looks at how much immigrants are committed to either their host country or their country of origin and classifies immigrants according to four states:

a) **assimilation:** The immigrant identifies strongly with the host culture and conforms to the norms, values and codes of conduct of the host country.
b) **integration:** The immigrant combines the cultural traditions of their home country with his commitment to the host country.
c) **marginalization:** The immigrant feels dedicated to neither culture.
d) **separation:** The immigrant is only committed to their country of origin although they might have lived abroad for many years and hardly take part in the culture of their host country.

c) Study the statistics resulting from a survey in 2018 carefully and interpret the figures. Use the language support in the box below.

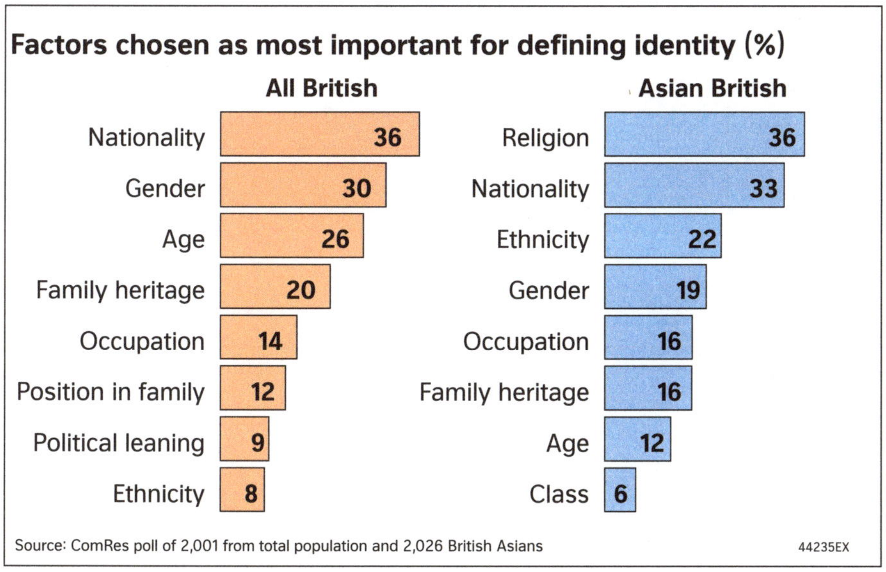

Language support

Analysing a chart / table

The chart taken from .... shows ... | It is striking ... | Compared to ... |
The numbers for ... are about twice as high as those ... | The numbers remain constant / steady |
The factors change clearly ... | By and large the statistics for ... reveal that ... | This clearly indicates that ... |
Against the backdrop of ..., the figures are (not) surprising / revealing / enlightening ...

d) **Group work (2-3)** Analyse how strongly the people in the memoir feel about their ethnic identity by studying the extracts below.

extracts	notes
Amolak:	
1. It was only when he referred to his appearance that Amolak's supernatural confidence disappeared; the turban, beard and moustache were a constant reminder of the chasm between how he saw himself and how others saw him. It also made his love of Bruce Springsteen's music seem hollow; Springsteen's songs were about being true to yourself and being the best you could be and yet it was only fear that was forcing my friend to retain his turban. When I saw Amolak clean-shaven and without his turban, at first I did not even recognise him. […] 'How's your dad taking it?' 'Not good,' he replied. Didn't talk to me when I got back from the barber, Mum didn't make me dinner ... they probably think I'm going to be bringing a white girl home next.' 'You're not that lucky,' I joked. 'Yeah, they'll get used to it. It's only hair for fuck's sake.' *(pp. 101-102)*	

extracts	notes
Mohammad Manzoor:	
2. My father was different from the men and women back in Pakistan: he had got out. In some ways my father was more English than he was Pakistani. He was like an Asian reincarnation of a traditional Victorian father: emotionally repressed; a strong belief in discipline and authority; faith in the value of hard work and education, and a disdain for excessive emoting. *(p. 251)*	
3. When my father had come to Britain in the sixties he had come as a Pakistani and he had died as a Pakistani; he had never wanted to be British. *(p. 265)*	
Sarfraz:	
4. I looked across at the relatives who were all chatting and laughing and listening to the wedding songs being played on the public address system. I thought these are my relatives, I am part of them and they are part of me. Some even looked like me. [...] In that instant I felt a sense of connection, a sense of being part of something bigger than my direct family I had not felt before. *(p. 73)*	
5. I had largely forgotten Arabic and the guilt for having lost the faith remained. [...] I wanted to believe and I hoped that by not drinking the possibility of a return to Islam still existed. So long as I did not touch alcohol then I could say I was a Muslim. It was not much of an identity but it was the only one that could not be denied to me. I was a Muslim. I just did not know what that meant. *(p. 231)*	
6. At the age of thirty I was comfortably British, occasionally Pakistani, and only technically Muslim. This was the twenty-first century after all. What did religion matter? *(p. 233)*	

extracts	notes
7. That was how I felt being Pakistani during the eighties: I wanted to be invisible and anonymous so that no one could point at me and say: 'You are different and you do not belong.' This country didn't seem to accept me as one of its own, and yet where else did I have that I could call home? Not Pakistan, which had felt completely alien to me. I didn't seem to belong anywhere. *(p. 255)*	
8. I had grown up in this country wanting to be British but I had never really felt as if I truly belonged here. *(p. 265)*	
Rasool Bibi:	
9. For my mother, it was home. I had never seen her happier; she was relaxed, smiling and seemed freer than in Luton. Back in Britain she hardly left the house, and when she did she was usually accompanied by my father. In Pakistan she would leave at nine or ten in the evening to visit a bazaar with a group of other women. When other women struck up conversations and asked her where she was from she would start by saying Faisalabad before slyly adding, 'But these days we live in England,' and this would promote a sharp intake of breath and wonderment. *(p. 250)*	
Sohail:	
10. What I had always found so infuriating about Sohail was, despite having spent thirty years in Britain, how Pakistani he was; his friends were all Pakistani and he remained resolutely unintegrated. Despite having been educated here his values were thoroughly traditional. My brother did not have any crisis of identity, he was not torn between two cultures. He was a Pakistani: [...] *(p. 86)*	

e) **Group work** Place the different people along the scale below and explain your decision.

assimilation ⟷ **separation**

8 CHOOSE

Write an essay about ethnic identity as portrayed in the book, in which you outline the people's attachment to their home or host country and explore the reasons for their attitude.

OR

Group work (6) Act out a talk show titled "Ethnic identity in Britain": Pick five students to step into the role of Sarfraz, Mohammad, Amolak, Rasool Bibi, and Sohail and another student for the talk show host. Host a talk show in which the host and the audience ask the characters questions about their ethnic identity. Use the information you have collected about the characters in task 4 and in your reading journal.

Growing up

9

a) **Pair work** Look at the situations below and pick the ones that are, used to be and probably will be important to you. Explain your choice to a partner.

hanging out with friends	having a job	playing with toys	having a family
going to church / mosque	visiting your family	choosing your partner	
succeeding at school	celebrating Christmas	deciding over your hair style	

b) **Group work** Find out how Sarfraz describes and assesses the situations above.

situations	notes
succeeding at school: *(p. 155, l. 14 to p. 157, l. 16)*	
playing with toys: *(p. 214, l. 26 to p. 215, l. 7)*	
deciding over your hair style: *(p. 43, l. 29 to p. 45, l. 5)*	
visiting family: *(p. 71, l. 27 to p. 73, l. 27)*	

situations	notes
hanging out with friends: *(p. 95, l. 20 to p. 96, l. 18)*	
having a job: *(p. 158, l. 26 to p. 165, l. 7)*	
choosing your partner: *(p. 185, l. 13 to p. 192, l. 4)*	
going to church / mosque: *(p. 221, l. 7 to p. 223, l. 21)*	
celebrating Christmas / Eid: *(p. 221, l. 7 to p. 222, l. 4)*	

c) Sarfraz Manzoor was in his thirties when he wrote *Greetings from Bury Park*. Find out what turn his life has taken ever since by studying the photo and the article. Research information about …

- finding the right partner.
- his wedding day.
- the reactions of his family.
- starting a family.

You can find a link to the article here:
Webcode DSW-73685-08

Discrimination in the UK

10

Sarfraz Manzoor describes how as a teenager he and other Asians were discriminated against.

a) **Pair work** Collect examples of harassment that Sarfraz and other Asians experienced.

page	examples (notes)
59	
119	
221	
251-254	

b) Although discrimination has become illegal, people still experience it in all sorts of places. Look at the advice given by different organizations on how to deal with discrimination.

1.	Focus on your core values, beliefs and personal strengths.
2.	Seek support systems such as family members, friends to share your experience with.
3.	Report to agencies or supervisors.
4.	Get involved with organizations or groups, e.g. online, to share your experiences with and learn how to address situations in the future.
5.	Help yourself think clearly before you react by slowing your breathing or using other relaxation exercises.
6.	Come up with a plan of how you could react differently next time.
7.	See professional help when you have symptoms of sadness or depression.

c) Choose the pieces of advice you find the most helpful.

d) **Pair work** Exchange your view with a partner.

e) Imagine you are Sarfraz seeking help from a school counsellor. Write their dialogue (As Sarfraz, tell the counsellor about the harassment you have experienced and how you feel. As the counsellor, try to come up with a plan that helps Sarfraz react more self-confidently the next time).

Arranged marriages

11

a) Describe how marriages are arranged in Sarfraz's family.

b) Explain what Sarfraz means when he says: "That was one of the problems with arranged marriages and importing husbands and wives from Pakistan: they thought marriage was a free ticket to an easy life." *(p. 68)*

c) Group work (4) Analyse the children's attitude towards arranged marriages. Each group member looks at a child (Sohail, Sarfraz, Navela or Uzma) more closely. Then share your results.

Sohail	Sarfraz	Navela	Uzma

d) A discussion → **S22** How to stage a debate

Group work (4-5) Stage a discussion between Pakistani parents and their British-born children. In preparation for this discussion collect arguments for and against arranged marriages. Consider ...

- social aspects,
- financial aspects,
- modern versus traditional ways of living.

CHOOSE

Group work (4-5) Now step into the roles of the mother, father, son and daughter. The discussion might be led by a friend of the family's or a matchmaker.

OR

Group work (3-5) Discuss to what extent the following quotation can be considered justified.

> "Have you ever heard of anyone from Pakistan getting divorced? It's impossible. We have more respect and we know that when you get married it is for the long term. When English people get married all they are thinking about is themselves but when Pakistanis get married they are thinking of their families and they are thinking of honour." *(p. 190)*

From Triangular slave trade to Presidency of the United States

1

a) Read the text below.
b) Pair work Write down four questions about the text to test your partner's knowledge.
c) Answer each other's questions.

With the permanent settlement in the New World of European colonists, the demand for raw materials like tobacco, cotton or sugar cane required an ever-growing number of workers. This was the dawn of **triangular slave trade**. The raw material was delivered from the New World to Europe where it was processed to textiles or other goods. These were brought to Africa. At the infamous **Slave Coast of West Africa** people were hunted down and then sold to European slave traders who displaced them to plantations in the West Indies (Caribbean) or the American South. It is estimated that more than 20 million Africans were sold as slaves – of which many did not even survive the deadly passage. The Atlantic slave trade lasted from the 17th to the 19th century, having its peak at the end of the 18th century and bringing upon an unthinkable suffering to the Africans.

Slavery was abholished in British colonies in 1838. The rising economic, social and political tensions in the United States led to the **American Civil War** from 1861 to 1865 in which the North led by U.S. President Abraham Lincoln emerged as the winning side bringing an end to slavery.

It took another hundred years, until 1955, for the *Civil Rights Movement* to take off and for individuals like Rosa Parks who refused to give up her seat for a white person, to fight back. This movement paved the way for a more equal treatment of black people. The March on Washington in 1963 where activist Dr. Martin Luther King delivered his famous "I have a dream" speech can be considered one of the most prominent events. Consequently, segregation was ended, African Americans were granted civil rights, and people of colour were allowed to attend white schools.

Yet, Dr. King's dream of full **emancipation** has still not been fulfilled. Still people of colour are massively disadvantaged: they are more likely to be scrutinized[1] by the police or even become victims of (police) violence. Originating in 2012 with the murder of an African American teenager named Trayvon Martin, the **Black Lives Matter** (BLM) movement became a worldwide phemomenon in 2020 when the murder of George Floyd was captured on camera while the police were arresting him. It denounces racial injustice and reminds us of the ghosts of the past (like the fact that there are still statues of slave traders or street names which honour people who benefitted from slavery).

Black Americans still have less oppurtunities to **climb the social ladder** largely due to having less acess to education. Former First Lady Michelle Obama called herself a rarity on campus at Princeton[2]. People of colour are more likely to become homeless, more likely to die from diseases like Covid-19. They are also less likely to have health insureance, they have a lower life expectancy, and on average they earn less. However there is a new generation of young black professionals who see current black people in positions of power as something to aspire to.

Barack Obama becoming the first black president from 2009 to 2017 or Kamala Harris the first woman in the position of vice president having African and Asian roots are landmarks for this new self-confidence. Nevertheless, there is still a long way to reach full emancipation.

Annotations
[1] to **be scrutinized** = to be checked, examined
[2] **Princeton** = a U.S. elite college

d) Explain the words printed in bold with one or two sentences.

Forms of racial discrimination

2

With the help of the text above and what you already know write down how people are discriminated against racially.

____

____

____

(Racial) discrimination

3

Read the following information about stereotypes, prejudices, discrimination and racism. What is your understanding of the terms? Discuss them in class and find examples.

Info

Stereotype, prejudice, discrimination and racism

The terms **stereotype** and **prejudice** are commonly used in everyday language. It is, however, not easy to define them and to differentiate them from each other. Generally speaking, stereotypes are generalizations about certain people or things. They are oversimplified ideas or images that emphasize certain traits or aspects in a way that distorts reality. A **prejudice** is a preconceived opinion or attitude that is not necessarily based on reason or actual experience.

Discrimination is often a consequence of existing stereotypes and prejudices. The term refers to the differential treatment of somebody because he / she belongs to a certain group. These groups are defined by factors such as race, gender or age. Discrimination is based on stereotypes or prejudices about the groups.

Racism is a concept which attributes certain character traits or characteristics to all people belonging to a certain "race". People who are racist consider some races superior to others. As a consequence, people belonging to a certain "race" may be discriminated against, which is called **racial discrimination**.

Stereotypes and **prejudices** are not necessarily negative in what they say about a group but can also express positive traits or characteristics associated with different groups. For example, the idea that Asians are good at maths and therefore better suited to working in the financial sector than others is a positive prejudice. This might lead bank managers to discriminate in favour of them when looking for new employees, which would be an example of **positive discrimination**.

4

a) Have you ever experienced a situation where you were or someone else was treated in a discriminating way? Write down the situation(s) taking notes. You may share your experience with your neighbour.

____

____

____

____

____

b) Pair work Discuss measures to prevent or intervene in racial discrimination. Write down dos and don'ts on a poster.

c) Collect and discuss the measures in class.

Cicada: a short story (2018)

PRE-READING

1

Describe the two pictures. Try to interpret in which situations the photos were taken and what the girls feel.

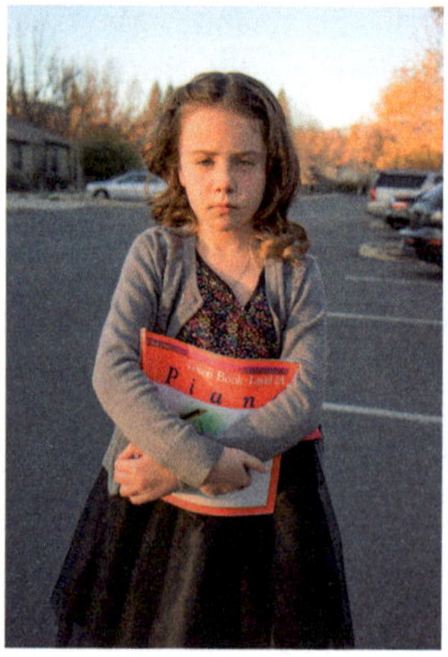

Info

Cicadas

The cicadas in the short story are an astonishing kind of bug that can be found in 15 states of the USA from Indiana to New York. Brood X only emerges from the ground to mate and die every 17 years in spring as soon as soil temperatures have risen to 18°C. Like a biblical plague there are billions of them, and streets, trees and houses are covered with millions of carcasses. The male cicadas are very loud and "sing" at almost 100 decibels. The phenomenon has been written about since the 18th century but it is estimated that the bugs have evolved their interesting life cycle since the Ice Age. Many people find the regular occurrence of the cicadas comforting and they see it as a chance to reflect on the passage of time whereas others try to protect themselves with umbrellas, stay at home or even evade them by going on holiday for the time they are there, which is two to six weeks until this episode is over.

Shells and carcasses of cicadas

2

After reading the info box and having looked at the picture – what sort of story would you expect with the title "Cicada"? What could it be about and what role could the insects play?

Cicada

by Camille Acker

In the dank[1] of DC's[2] summer heat, cicadas scaled[3] the heights of oak trees, vocal[4] and untrained trapeze artists. But their shells[5], discarded[6] and crumpled like candy wrappers, clogged[7] drains[8] and littered the sides of the road.

The air was smeared[9] with humidity[10], but as they drove through Rock Creek Park, a breeze[11] lifted and Ellery, her face thrust out of the car window, waited for the wind to hopscotch[12] across her cheeks.

"Stop." Her mother tugged[13] on Ellery's elbow and Ellery lowered her face back into the interior of Ms. Anita's car.

"Lo, she's fine." Her father turned around from the passenger seat. He frowned at her mother and winked[14] at Ellery.

"All these damn bugs[15]. Devils, I tell you," Ms. Anita said. The wheels[16] of her car crushed the dark masses again and again.

On the playground at Ellery's school, a boy picked up one of the cracked bodies and threw it at the long, full ponytail of a girl. She tried to shake free of it, catching the Holy Ghost far from the aisles[17] of any church, like the one Ellery's mother dragged her to on Sundays. "Get it out! Get it off!" the girl yelled[18]. The giggling[19] bunch[20] of boys ran, but Ellery, with her thumb and forefinger, pulled the bug remains out of the strands of hair.

"My science teacher says they wait underground until they're ready to come out," Ellery said. She tried to lean forward between the seats, but the seat belt[21] pulled her back.

"Your dress," her mother said. She brushed non-existent bits of lint[22] from the fabric, stiff[23] from dry cleaning. Her mother had insisted that would make it look best for today. It didn't smell like it had been cleaned, not like their clothes after they washed them at the laundromat[24]. Their dryer at home had been broken since last summer. Their washing machine had stopped at Christmas.

"You go all this way for her to take piano?" Ms. Anita asked. "I bet there's somebody right over in Northeast."

"You're probably right, Ms. Anita," Mom answered back. She had to yell so her voice would land on the waiting ears of Ms. Anita instead of the wind taking it out to the trees.

"Too much money over here, you ask me," Ms. Anita said.

"Appreciate this ride, especially today. All of these rides you've given us. We could have just taken the bus – "

"Probably have to take two different ones to get you this far west of the park."

"Three," her mother said, but this time she did not yell.

The kids in her neighborhood all hated being west of the park: Woodley Park or Friendship Heights or Ellery's favorite neighborhood (the site of her piano lessons, the site of today's excitement), the Gold Coast. Ellery had no name for the collection of streets around her home where she skinned[25] knees and hands. The houses on the Gold Coast weren't just in rows, obedient[26] toy soldiers. These houses were like gathering up all the toys Ellery had ever owned, the Barbies, the stuffed animals, the building blocks. They had what her mother called turrets[27] or Juliet balconies[28] and front yards[29] big enough for a good game of tag[30]. Even the plain brick[31] ones caused a tightness in Ellery's belly. Some of them had ivy[32] growing up the sides, angling[33] for a way in.

"I don't know how you've been making it without a car –"

"We've been making it fine," her father said.

"Even to the Gold Coast?" Ms. Anita asked. Her father said that Ms. Anita wouldn't believe you even if you said water was wet. When Ellery went over to use Ms. Anita's piano to practice, she would always ask how long it'd be.

"Just an hour, Ms. Anita," her mother told her. "About the same time it would take me to do your hair." And then, Ms. Anita, putting a hand to her gelled ponytail, would say, "Well, if it's just an hour . . ."

"Mom, look," Ellery said. "I bet it's cool in there." She reached out to grip her mother's forearm without turning to see where her fingers would land. Ellery could feel drops of sweat down her back[34] like her mother pouring

Annotations

1 **dank** = wet
2 **DC** = Washington DC: capital of the United States
3 to **scale** = to climb on
4 **vocal** = concerning the voice
5 **shell** = here: body
6 to **discard** = to throw away
7 to **clog** = to block
8 **drain** = place where rainwater disappears on a road; *Gully*
9 to **be smeared** = to be spread around
10 **humidity** = wetness
11 **breeze** = *Lüftchen, Brise*
12 to **hopscotch** = to travel (reference to a children's game called hopscotch where you jump around)
13 to **tug** = to pull
14 to **wink** = to blink with just one eye
15 **bug** = insect
16 **wheel** = A car drives on four wheels.
17 **aisle** = a walkway in a church between rows of seats
18 to **yell** = to scream
19 to **giggle** = to laugh
20 **bunch** = group
21 **seat belt** = Because it is too dangerous it is not allowed to drive a car without a seat belt on.
22 **lint** = tiny piece of fabric (wool, cotton etc)
23 **stiff** = inflexible
24 **laundromat** = place where you can wash dirty clothes
25 to **skin** = to injure slightly
26 **obedient** = to follow all the rules
27 **turret** = *Balkon in Form eines Türmchens*
28 **Juliet balcony** = small / French balcony with windows down to the floor
29 **front yard** = a garden at the front of a house
30 **game of tag** = a game where you chase and try to touch sb else
31 **brick** = type of (red) stone houses are made of
32 **ivy** = plant that often grows on houses
33 to **angle** = to aim at sth
34 **back** = *Rücken*

water over her head in the kitchen sink[35] when she got her hair washed, the towel[36] on her neck already good and soaked[37]. The wetness now the stickiness[38] of salt, not the stickiness of conditioner.

"So, this a recital[39]?" Ms. Anita asked. She watched for the answer in her rearview mirror, waiting for Ellery's mother to respond.

"No, it's a competition. Mrs. Hamilton says that's like a recital with prizes," Ellery answered before her mother could.

"Oh yeah? You gonna win?" Ms. Anita asked. She jutted an elbow out to Ellery's father and smiled.

"Yes," Ellery said. When she played the piano, Ellery could find no edges to the world, no start and stop. Not in the music or in the Italian words Mrs. Hamilton used to tell Ellery to slow down or play loudly. The world was there for her. She was just waiting to come out and see it.

Ms. Anita's car clunked into the circular driveway of the recital hall. It was really a kind of church, a synagogue, her father told them.

"Pretty slick, huh?" Dad said. But Ellery wouldn't have called the building slick, not like the shine on the escalators in the Metro. The white building trimmed[40] in the silver of its four large columns was more like the platter they used only for Thanksgiving and Christmas dinner. Ellery was never allowed to carry it to the table or even pick it up when she served herself turkey[41]. Ms. Anita rounded the corners of the drive and braked[42] her old car in front of the large wooden doors of the synagogue. The cicadas were quieter here.

"Ready?" her father asked. He craned[43] around to smile at Ellery in the back seat. The armpits of his white shirt were already soake through with sweat. Her mother rubbed her back and Ellery nodded.

"You sure you won't come, Ms. Anita?" Mom asked.

"Got my book club," Ms. Anita said. "But you call me and I'll come back."

Her father opened the car door and Ellery climbed out, trying to keep her legs together like her mother always said, but she couldn't get out of the car like that. She jumped out and landed with a hop on the sidewalk. She made sure not to turn in case disapproval was on her mother's face. Her father grabbed one of her hands, her mother the other, and they walked toward the building. Ms. Anita's car creaked away[44] behind them.

The four doors before them were the dark wood of the banister[45] at Grandma's house that Mom always told her was not meant for messing[46]. Glass above the wood reflected their three bodies back to them, but it would have taken at least six Ellerys stacked[47] on one another for her to reach the top. In the white stone above the glass, somebody had carved two candleholders and one picture of a book with round corners instead of pointy ones. It was better than any Gold Coast house she'd ever seen. Her father tugged at her hand to get her through one of the doors.

Inside, the ceilings stretched even higher than the glass. It would take even more Ellerys to reach the top. Her shoes echoed on the synagogue's stone floor; each sole striking as if someone were bouncing a ball.

"Sure feels nice in here," Dad said. He wiped his brow[48] with his free hand.

The outstretched arms of smiling women with flowers pinned to the front of their clothes directed them to a red carpeted area in front of more doors. Now, Ellery's shoes couldn't be heard at all, as if she had vanished[49]. There was just one door this time, wide and wooden. Her father grabbed a silver handle[50] and opened it for Ellery to walk through. Her mother held her hand even tighter as if they were about to cross the street.

At the front of this new room, the one where she would perform, was the same rounded book, but bigger and lit up, maybe from a spotlight somewhere Ellery couldn't see. Ellery and her mother belonged to a congregation[51] that was small and, as her father said, too broke[52] to worship anywhere better than a high school cafeteria. The sanctuary[53] was a bunch of metal folding chairs and tables that sometimes had dried ketchup on them. It always smelled of newly opened cans[54] of corn[55].

Here, the air was like right after her mother vacuumed[56] the carpet. There were no worn-out tables, the ones at the front too beautiful for anybody to ever be allowed to get ketchup near them. Four steps led up to the stage, glowing from the light of the big book and from the gleam[57] of polished[58] wood. To the left side was all that mattered, a piano: grand, white, and gleaming. It was not the old upright[59] at Ms. Anita's or the kind at Mrs. Hamilton's, smaller than this one and black.

[35] **sink** = place where dishes are cleaned by hand
[36] **towel** = A towel is needed to dry sth.
[37] to **be soaked** = to be extremely wet
[38] **stickiness** = *Klebrigkeit*
[39] **recital** = here: a concert
[40] to **be trimmed** = *verziert*
[41] **turkey** = bird typically served for Thanksgiving in the US
[42] to **brake** = to go slower
[43] to **crane** = to stretch one's neck
[44] to **creak away** = to drive off slowly making a noise

[45] **banister** = you can often hold your hand for support on a banister when going up or down stairs
[46] to **mess** = to make dirty
[47] to **be stacked** = to be placed on top of each other
[48] **brow** = part of the face above the eyes
[49] to **vanish** = When sth that once was there, goes away suddenly.
[50] **handle** = You open a door by using the handle.
[51] **congregation** = a group of religious people in a church
[52] to **be broke** = to have run out of money
[53] **sanctuary** = a safe place
[54] **can** = Food is sold in this metal container.
[55] **corn** = a tall vegetable plant with yellow grains
[56] to **vacuum** = to clean the floor using an electric device
[57] **gleam** = a pale light
[58] to **be polished** = to be made shiny
[59] **upright** = a type of piano

Mrs. Hamilton descended[60] from her place on the stage. Her long brown hair was piled[61] on top of her head in a bun[62]. Ellery's mother wore her hair in a bun like that some times, but only when she didn't care what her hair looked like. At the stove when she was cooking. When they carried laundry baskets full of clothes to the laundromat. Mrs. Hamilton wasn't about to do laundry or cook a pot of spaghetti. Her hair was messy on purpose. And even though her dress sparkled, golden threads woven into the swirls of deep pink and white, Mrs. Hamilton didn't look dressed up.

"And you're here," Mrs. Hamilton said. Even words that weren't Italian Mrs. Hamilton said as though they were. She had lived in Europe, she told Ellery often. All over Europe. One place in Europe would have been plenty for Ellery, but that it was more than one seemed important to Mrs. Hamilton. Mrs. Hamilton shook Mom's and Dad's hands, clasping[63] their one hand with both of hers, ringed and nail polished. "The parents may sit anywhere they like. Closer is better of course to see the beautiful finger work Signorina Ellery will do."

Her father scanned the half-filled cushioned movie theater seats. "Space right there." He grabbed Ellery's shoulder and shook it. "You'll do great."

"It'll be beautiful. I already know," her mother said. She fished for a comb[64] in her purse[65] and fussed over the front of Ellery's hair. She leaned back to check her work and smiled. Baby powder peeked out from the neckline of her mother's black dress. If Ellery touched it, the whiteness would only spread.

Her father jingled[66] the change in his pocket. "Come on, we don't want to lose those seats."

Her mother stroked[67] Ellery's hair again. Dad put a hand on her back and led her away.

"Shall we meet your competition?" Mrs. Hamilton said. The other students, some boys, mostly girls, were seated in the first row. A few of them only nodded at her as Mrs. Hamilton went down the line naming those she knew and prompting others to introduce themselves. "Have a seat here." Mrs. Hamilton gestured to an empty seat between two girls, both in cropped[68], colorful sweaters and spring dresses. Both had stud earrings[69], and one, when she touched a hand to her tortoiseshell[70] headband, revealed a silver bracelet[71] with a tiny silver tag[72] hanging from it. They sat with their ankles crossed and their hands picking at starched[73] sundress collars[74]. These girls got out of cars with their legs together and their shoes unscuffed[75].

"I'm Cara," the girl without the bracelet said when Ellery sat down. She wasn't nearly as pretty as the other girl. Mrs. Hamilton clicked away from them in her high heels.

"I'm Ellery," she said. She turned to smile at the other girl too, the one with the bracelet, even though she hadn't yet given her name.

"I like your hair," the girl said. She pulled on her blond ponytail, resting it on her shoulder.

Ellery's hair had been pressed that morning. She had begged[76] her mother for months to let her cut it. She would be in junior high[77] soon, she told her, couldn't she be just a little grown now? Her mother finally cut it when she knew Ellery would be in the competition. Ellery felt the ends of her hair and smiled at her.

"I wish my hair were fuller like that. Mine is so fine and lays so flat, but you've got that kind of poof[78] at your roots.[79]" The girl widened her eyes when she said *poof*.

Ellery nodded. She felt an ache somewhere her arms were too short to reach.

"Lori!" Cara whisper-shouted before she let escape a small laugh. Her voice snapped to pity when Ellery's hand went to the front of her hair. "She's just like that," Cara assured her.

Lori probably cheated at war and ate all the red Now and Laters[80] in the pack. Lori might have lived in one of those houses that Ellery loved, but she wouldn't last one minute with an alley-glass-skinned knee[81]. She'd have gone home crying to her mother. She wouldn't have gotten right back on her bike and kept riding.

One of the other white women besides Mrs. Hamilton quieted the crowd. Her fingers pressed down on the air as if she were playing all the keys of the piano at once. Ellery turned to search for the faces of her parents, but she could no longer tell, even in the swarm of white bodies, which bodies she belonged to. She thought she saw her mother's hair between the gelled heads of two suited white men, but when she leaned her head back to make sure, Lori hissed at her.

"Your teacher's looking at you. You better pay attention," Lori said. Ellery tilted forward[82], sitting straighter in her seat so she wouldn't disappoint Mrs. Hamilton. When she glanced Mrs. Hamilton's way though, she wasn't watching Ellery, only the stage. "Maybe she was looking

[60] to **descend** = to go down
[61] to **be piled** = to put things on top of each other
[62] **bun** = You can wear long hair in a ponytail or twisted in a round bun.
[63] to **clasp** = to hold sth tight
[64] **comb** = You use this item with a row of teeth to go through your hair and get it tidy.
[65] **purse** = wallet
[66] to **jingle** = to make a sound like bells ringing
[67] to **stroke** = to move gently with your hand
[68] **cropped** = to wear sth which is so short that the belly can be seen
[69] **stud earrings** = you wear them in your ears; *Ohrenstecker*
[70] **tortoiseshell** = in the pattern of the outer part of a tortoise
[71] **bracelet** = jewellery worn around the arm
[72] **tag** = *Anhänger*
[73] to **be starched** = to be made inflexible
[74] **sundress collar** = a light summer dress and the collar is the part around the neck
[75] to **be unscuffed** = to be clean and not worn down
[76] to **beg** = to plead for sth because you want it very much
[77] **Junior high** = in general classes 7 to 9
[78] **poof** = big or voluminous hair
[79] **root** = The origin of hair is situated in the roots.
[80] **Now and Later** = an American brand of fruit-flavored candy which is formed into squares packaged in colorful paper[1]
[81] **alley-glass-skinned knee** = an injury on the leg from glass in a narrow street
[82] to **tilt forward** = to move forward with (part of) your body

somewhere else," Lori said. She shrugged her shoulders.

Ellery placed her folded hands in her lap just like Lori and tried to hold her knees together through the songs of the youngest kids, all of the tunes short, in four-four time, and played allegro, joyful and fast.

Finally, Ellery's age group began to play. Each pianist (Mrs. Hamilton said Ellery should call herself that) in their turn going up to the stage, having their piece announced, and then setting off, waiting for their fingers to remember all the movements that had been drilled into them for weeks. Some of them had played in competitions before, Mrs. Hamilton told her at her lessons. But it didn't mean they were any better than her and even those who had won had no advantage: "Winning once doesn't mean you will win again," Mrs. Hamilton said.

Lori went up to play and Ellery let her knees go limp[83] and her ankles uncross. A woman announced the title of Lori's piece and before she sat at the bench[84], Lori raised a shoulder and a smile for the audience, who complimented this preperformance with louder applause than the girl before her had received at the end of her song. From head to toe, Lori was a new Mary Jane shoe[85] fresh out of the box, buffed[86] to a shine so you could see your own reflection in it, but all lopsided[87] and weird. The squeeze and hurt of it. Still, Ellery also longed for pretty things. She clapped[88], but with her hands still in her lap.

The Italian words resounded in Loris playing. *Forte* when it should be. *Piano* when it was best. Lori might really know those words, maybe she had been all over Europe like Mrs. Hamilton. Lori's finger positioning was precise, her hands arched[89] as if tennis balls rested under her palms. It was the way Mrs. Hamilton wanted Ellery to play, but Ellery's hands sometimes fell a little flat, perched[90] too low.

"Hey," Cara said, poking[91] Ellery's still-folded hands. From the side of the stage, this time Mrs. Hamilton was looking at her and motioning with both hands for Ellery to come. Standing, Ellery would have the best chance to see her parents, but looking behind her might mean tripping over[92] something. She walked toward Mrs. Hamilton, never turning around and with her hands clasped in front of her.

"Go up and wait." Mrs. Hamilton gently pushed at Ellery's back. She walked up the three steps to the stage, concealed[93] from the audience by velvet[94] curtains. Ellery could focus on Lori's face now, the way she couldn't sitting right next to her. Her nose was smaller than Ellery's. Her cheeks the pink of watermelon candy, a color that would have been muted on Ellery's dark skin. Lori's ponytail flounced[95] as she played, as excited to be there with her as the rest of the audience was. She was pretty good, but maybe church just made music better.

Sometimes on Sundays, Ellery's mother would raise a hand and wave it during a song. Once after service, Ellery asked her why she did that. All her mother would say is that she felt full. Ellery thought of the discomfort of too many hamburgers or one scoop too many of ice cream, but her mother's full – a hand at her heart and the dots of tears at the corners of her eyes– was different. "All I feel just comes out," she told Ellery.

Lori finished, and when she rose from the bench and bowed, the audience clapped happily. Three people in the front wrote on sheets of paper, the judges, she now remembered Mrs. Hamilton whispering to her on the walk to her seat. A row of well-dressed white people stood up, clapping louder than the rest. Lori exited the stage and came toward Ellery. Lori looked like she might speak, but only poked her lips out at Ellery and pulled her wandering ponytail back to its place on her shoulder.

The woman announced Ellery's piece and extended her hand to invite Ellery to start playing. Ellery moved out of the shadows of the curtains and stood before the audience. She started to bow, but she did it slowly hoping during her bending she would finally see her parents, but she couldn't find them. She wasn't even sure where her own seat was anymore. The distance from her to the piano grew, but Ellery imagined this was Ms. Anita's house, the same shaky wooden bench, the same smell of bleach[96] and Vaseline, her mother just starting on Ms. Anita's hair.

Ellery sat at the keys and placed the tips of her fingers on the ivories[97]. She lightly stroked them. Then, she finally pressed down and played the opening chord[98]. She loved the way it sounded. Her fingers raced across the keys to the next chord. *Too fast*, she heard Mrs. Hamilton say in her head as she would in practice. Ellery slowed and pressed each note so every one would be heard. She chanted[99] Italian words, whispering them to herself. Most had nothing to do with her song, but the melody of them made her want to do her best. The notes played well together, and those notes led to new notes, which led to other notes. Ellery didn't know if this piano was better or if this church, this synagogue, where music played that made people feel full, was doing the same for her music, but she felt it. She felt full. Or maybe she felt just out of the dirt, out from underground and into the summer sun.

[83] to **go limp** = to relax
[84] **bench** = a seat for one or two people normally made of wood
[85] **Mary Jane shoe** = Jane which have shoes made by the company named Mary Jane have a strap with flat heels.
[86] to **be buffed** = to be polished
[87] to **be lopsided** = to be unequal
[88] to **clap** = to give applause
[89] to **arch** = to move a part of your body so that it makes a curve
[90] to **perch** = to hold
[91] to **poke** = to touch quickly
[92] to **trip over sth** = to fall over sth
[93] to **be concealed** = to be hidden
[94] **velvet** = a luxurious soft material

[95] to **flounce** = to move abruptly
[96] **bleach** = a chemical used to make sth become white(r)
[97] **ivory** = Elephants' teeth are made of this substance.
[98] **chord** = Two or more notes are played together.
[99] to **chant** = to sing (again and again)

She touched the last of the notes, her fingers light on them, *piano*, and then off of them and back into her lap.

She heard the clapping before she stood up all the way, before she turned around and took her bow. And then she saw them, her parents standing up like Lori's had. Her father yelling and calling out her name. Her mother wasn't clapping, but she had a hand to her heart. Cara was waiting to play and could only stare at Ellery. At the bottom of the three stairs, Mrs. Hamilton leaned toward Ellery and touched the side of her face. "Beautiful," she told her. Ellery smiled. Some people were still clapping, some people who weren't even her parents. Ellery walked back to her seat. Lori didn't say anything, didn't even give her a smile. Ellery sat and Cara played, but even though the room was filled with as much sound as before, Ellery heard nothing over the thump of her heartbeat.

They announced the winners for the younger kids first, the third prize and the second. The first-prize winner, a boy with blue pants, a pinstriped[100] shirt, and a bowtie[101], ran up when they called his name. His parents took pictures, and he smiled and posed until they said he could stop. The woman who had introduced all of them stepped back to the microphone after the little boy finally left the stage. She thanked everyone for coming and then began to thank a long list of other people.

"You were really good," Cara whispered to Ellery.

Ellery smiled, but didn't thank her, wary of daggers of giggles[102] that might follow.

"Any *thing* can make noise," Lori said.

"You were really good, like really good," Cara said again without a giggle or a smile to diminish[103] her words.

"For our nine-to-twelve age group, we had some excellent competitors representing many parts of the city. Our judges had a difficult task, but we chose three pianists we think excelled[104] today."

She paused, and Ellery didn't want to hope too hard that her name would come out of her mouth. "In third place and winning one hundred dollars, Bobby McMillan."

From the other side of the crowd, a boy Ellery hadn't even remembered playing went up. He shook the woman's hand up and down and up and down until she took her hand away to give him two stiff pieces of paper, a certificate and a check.

"And, in second place, with a piece that showed real technique by a pianist who exhibited great poise[105] – that's the importance of this competition too, not just playing music, but turning these kids into true ladies and gentlemen."

Ellery didn't know if she had been ladylike enough for this woman or if she had "great poise."

"Our second-place prize of two hundred fifty dollars goes to Lori Hansen."

"See," Lori breathed out before she went forward to claim her trophy and check. She curtsied[106] for the audience and they clapped harder.

Lori came back to Ellery's side and hissed, "Can't imagine you'll be able to top that."

"And our first-prize winner in our nine-to-twelve age group is someone who really surprised the judges . . ."

The woman stopped, building urgency, and Ellery knew her mother was in the audience saying to her father, "Why don't she get on with it?" Ellery wanted her to, but then she didn't because she might not have won and then she would have to turn to this girl next to her and say something about her winning, not because she really wanted to, but because she would want her to know her parents had taught her well.

Ellery took in a deep breath to either help her say "Thank you" to the judges or "Congratulations" to Lori.

"The winner is Ellery Cook."

Ellery heard a squeal[107] from the audience. She walked up the steps of the stage and to the waiting woman. The fullness of playing multiplied, winning all the marbles in a game of jacks[108], seeing a tree full of cicadas where it seemed at first there was just one. The trophy was just a note, a musical note, mounted on a stone stand, but on that stand were the words *First Place*. But what Ellery really wanted was the $500 check.

The woman smiled and handed it to her. "Congratulations."

Ellery didn't shake her hand like the boy had and she didn't curtsy. Her smile and thank-you were so small, they ended up being only for herself. She descended the stairs of the stage to more congratulations and compliments on her playing. Everyone was standing up, kids finding their parents and parents finding their joyous or disappointed child.

Lori and Cara were just past the last step. Ellery fingered her first-place trophy and Lori fingered the careful pleats[109] of her dress.

"Winning is just for fun," Lori said.

"It was fun," Ellery said. "How I won."

The watermelon candy at Lori's cheeks darkened.

Out of the clusters of people, Ellery's parents emerged[110]. Her father whooping[111] and letting loose emphatic one-word sentences. "Yes." "Right." "Winner." Ellery could see from her mother's swollen eyes that she had been crying.

[100] **pinstriped** = a cloth with a vertical white line on dark background often used for business suits
[101] **bowtie** = a strip of cloth that is tied in the same way you tie shoes and worn around the collar for formal events
[102] **daggers of giggles** = *Lachsalven*
[103] to **diminish** = to milden
[104] to **excel** = to be exceptionally good at sth
[105] **poise** = a confident attitude
[106] to **curtsy** = to bend one's knees in front of an important person
[107] **squeal** = to make a long high sound
[108] to **win the marbles in a game of jacks** = to win all the awards
[109] **pleat** = *Falten*
[110] to **emerge** = to appear
[111] to **whoop** = to cheer

"This one," Mrs. Hamilton said, floating toward them and pointing at Ellery, "did magnificently[112] well."

"We thought so too," Dad said. He patted Ellery's head, mussing her hair until she allowed a smile to escape.

"It was so beautiful. The song," her mother said. "I've heard her play it, but — "

"She played it better today than she ever has," Mrs. Hamilton said. "You like your prize?"

Ellery nodded, renewing her grip on the trophy. She moved away from her parents so she could present the check. She wanted to do it just like the lady on the lottery drawing. "Here. It's for the car. We won't have to take the bus," Ellery said. She unfolded her arm and let the peach-colored paper dangle[113] from her fingertips.

Her mother glanced at Mrs. Hamilton and then squatted down[114] in front of Ellery. She placed her hand under one curled[115] side of Ellery's hair. "Honey, it's a savings bond[116]."

The bond was stiffer than cash or a check, but Ellery didn't know why that made a difference. She searched her father's face for the answer.

"See, baby, that number it has? That five hundred? Well, it's worth something it's not really worth yet. But by the time you go to college, by then, what it says it's worth, it'll be worth," her father said.

"Don't you worry about a car. This is yours," her mother said. She pushed Ellery's hair behind her ear, only to pull it back out again. Grooming[117] her even though her moment was over.

"Oh." Ellery dropped the hand with the bond down to her side.

"You kind of have to believe it'll get to be worth that in time," her father said. He put a hand on Mom's back and she straightened back to her height. Ellery looked no one in the eye.

"You won, remember?" Mrs. Hamilton said, her voice in a sharp key. "Smile."

They waited in the circular driveway for Ms. Anita to come. From the trees, the cicadas were deafening[118] the street, before they would be gone for seventeen more years. By then, Ellery would be grown and the $500 savings bond would finally be worth its face value[119]. Her parents chattered along with the cicadas. They told her how proud they were and how beautiful her playing was. Mom couldn't wait to tell the other members of the choir, and Dad couldn't wait to tell everybody he knew.

Lori and her family came out through the dark, wooden doors. Ellery tightened her grip on the trophy and savings bond. The people who had stood up and cheered for Lori surrounded her now. Two men in suits and two ladies in grown-up versions of the dress Lori had on. The group walked around Ellery's family, but Lori came closer than the others, brushing past Ellery's mother, her pink cashmere cardigan nudging[120] the polyester of her mother's dress. Her mother turned toward Lori and her family.

"Congratulations," Lori said. The family members nodded their approval of Lori's word.

"Say thank you, Ellery," her mother said. Ellery squeezed her mother's hand, but did not speak. Her mother smiled at Lori and found the faces of the adults. "Your daughter. She was wonderful."

"Yes, thank you." The woman had Lori's face, but no watermelon candy at her cheeks. Hair that might once have been pulled into a coveted[121] ponytail lay on her shoulders, straightened and brightly blond. On one wrist was a bracelet with the same small tag that Lori's had and a ring with a stone so far from her finger it seemed suspended[122] in midair. Her dress looked as if it had been dry-cleaned. No sweat ringed her underarms. There was no baby powder to be found.

"That dress is very pretty," her mother said. She always knew how much things cost without looking at price tags[123]. "Slow down," she would tell Ellery, "don't splash water on that lady," she might say, "that dress cost her good money." "Don't kick that dirt up around that man, his suit is more than I make in a week."

"Thank you." The woman took Lori's hand and turned away from Ellery's mother.

They walked to a car nearby, silver like the synagogue's columns. The car's horn[124] beeped and one of the men opened the front door for the woman holding Lori's hand. The man opened the door for Lori next. Lori turned back and smiled. Her teeth were so straight, white fence posts lined up and freshly painted. She smoothed out[125] the back of her skirt and sat down. The man closed the door behind her and all Ellery could see of Lori through the window was the pink of her face and the blond of her ponytail.

"Now, that's a beautiful thing right there. Never seen that model in that color," her father said. He leaned down and said very near Ellery's ear, "One day soon, we'll be riding in that."

Other car doors closed, slammed[126]. The cicadas only got louder.

Lori's car started to take off, going around the circular driveway of the synagogue. Ellery dropped her mother's

[112] **magnificent** = brilliant
[113] to **dangle** = to hang
[114] to **squat down** = to sit on your heels
[115] **curled** = the opposite of straight hair is curled hair
[116] **savings bond** = *Sparbrief*
[117] to **groom** = to make neat / tidy
[118] to **be deafening** = to make so much noise that you almost hear nothing else
[119] **face value** = real worth
[120] to **nudge** = to touch
[121] **coveted** = desired
[122] to **be suspended** = to be hanging
[123] **price tag** = here: small card with the price on
[124] **car horn** = A driver uses a car horn to make a noise and thus alarm others.
[125] to **smooth sth out** = to make flat
[126] to **slam** = to close quickly with a noise

hand and walked toward the departing car, quickening her steps when the wheels began to spin faster. When her legs couldn't keep up, she bent down and picked up the shells of the cicadas, pushed to the side in gutters[127] and broken under indifferent[128] wheels. She hurled the black bodies at the windows of the car. She ran now, her Mary Janes pinching[129]. She picked up more cicada shells, throwing two or three at a time and then three or four more. She threw all the shells she could find, even when the car pulled out of the driveway. She was breathing fast by the time she stopped running at the end of the drive, still holding a couple of cicada shells in her hand. She walked back toward the synagogue, turning around as she went to see how far away the car was.

"Did you see?" Ellery asked her parents. Ellery breathed out and smiled. "Did you?"

[127] **gutter** = where water is collected in a channel at the edge of a road
[128] **indifferent** = not caring
[129] to **pinch** = to hurt

WHILE READING

Characterization

3

a) Take an informed guess of how old Ellery is. Prove with the text.

Info

Always keep the two different forms of characterization in a literary text in mind.

direct characterization
The reader is told directly and explicitly about the character by the narrator or the characters
(Example: "(Cara) wasn't nearly as pretty as the other girl." p. 61, l. 215)

indirect characterization
The reader learns about the chracter's traits indirectly by reading between the lines (character's actions, looks, clothes or language).
(Example: "Ellery had no name for the collection of streets around her home where she skinned knees and hands." p. 59, ll. 53-54) ➡ She still plays games outside in which she gets dirty.

b) **Pair work** What do we learn about Ellery's family at the beginning of the short story (pp. 59-60, ll. 1-111)? Characterize Ellery's parents. Also consider their social background.

→ **S12** Checklist: Analysis – prose

Tip You can find aspects of characterization in *Camden Town Oberstufe* p. 244.

Features of a short story

4

Short stories often follow a certain scheme. Look at the main elements and features of short stories. Fill in the grid for "Cicada":

A short story	"Cicada"
1. ... has got an exposition or quickly throws the reader into the story without a lot of explanations.	
2. ... has got a theme.	
3. ... focuses on one or two protagonist(s) / antagonist(s).	
4. ... may have further characters.	

A short story	"Cicada"
5. ... has a single or limited setting.	
6. ... is less complex and has a limited plot.	[redacted]
7. ... mostly includes a conflict.	
8. ... has not got a lot of development.	
9. ... has got a climax.	
10. ... has an open-ending.	
11. ... has a limited number of words.	*It has about 5000 words.*
12. ... has no chapters.	
13. ... has not got a lot of development of the characters. However, the story depicts an important moment in the characters' lives.	
14. ... needs to be read twice to dive deeper into it and should be read between the lines. (Give example(s).)	

5

a) The story could be split up into different parts. Give each part a suitable heading.

ll. 1-122 ______________________

ll. 123-200 ______________________

ll. 201-261 ______________________

ll. 262-486 ______________________

ll. 487-562 ______________________

b) Take notes, then summarize the story.

Checklist

How to write a summary

- ✓ Start with an introductory sentence in which you name the author, the name of the story, the time of publication, a rough outline of the action and the theme.
- ✓ Use your own words.
- ✓ Use the present tense.
- ✓ Focus on the most important information.
- ✓ Don't use direct speech and do not quote.

POST-READING

Point of view

6

Identify the point of view (narrative perspective) and explain what consequence the choice of narrative perspective has on the reader. → **S2** Checklist creative writing

7 Think-Pair-Share

a) **Think** When do we learn about Ellery's and Lori's skin colour? What consequence does this have for the story and its dramatic structure?

b) **Pair** Exchange your ideas with a partner.

c) **Share** Present your ideas to the class.

8

a) Tick (✓) the boxes to finish the sentence. More than one solution is possible. Explain your choice.
The story "Cicada" ...

1. grabs attention with suspense. ❑ a conflict. ❑ a mystery. ❑ a character being in action. ❑
2. provides insight into a character's motivation. ❑ a character's fears or beliefs. ❑ the world. ❑ life. ❑ truth. ❑ justice. ❑ reality. ❑
3. has a predictable ending. ❑ has a surprising ending. ❑ has a resolved ending. ❑

b) **Pair work** Comment on the emotions the story may have evoked in you.

9

a) Describe Ellery's and Lori's relationship from the moment they meet (l. 205) until the end of the story. Explain Ellery's and Lori's feelings towards each other.

b) **Group work** Comment on Ellery's behaviour at the end of the story.

10 CHOOSE

Now, with all the information from the tasks above characterize Ellery **OR** Lori.

a) Write down your notes in the following table or on an extra sheet of paper.

aspect	quote	interpretation
1. outward appearance physical features / clothes / body language		
2. character traits e.g. modesty, courage, uncertainty		
3. behaviour How a character acts, gives an impression of his / her motives, abilities or moral standing.		
4. mood the emotional state of a character		
5. language correct or incorrect use of grammar, simple or sophisticated vocabulary, colloquial language; reflects a character's social background, education, attitudes, etc.		
6. family / social background		
7. relationship with others how a character interacts with others and is perceived by them		

b) Now write a coherent text supported with quotations from the short story.

→ **S12** Checklist: Analysis – prose

→ **S23** How to quote

Language support

Writing a characterization

The protagonist is described as (being)...

The fact that he / she ... reveals that...

He or she seems to be...

... shows / proves that he or she is ...

... appears to be... / ... is portrayed as...

Atmosphere

11

a) Read the useful adjectives to describe an atmosphere and fill in the grid below. Look up the ones you don't know.

anxious | cheerful | chilly | cold | cosy | depressing | desperate | discomforting | eerie | exciting | formal | funny | gloomy | happy | hostile | light-hearted | lively | peaceful | peculiar | playful | relaxed | romantic | sad | scary | spooky | staggering | stiff | suspenseful | tense | terrifying | uncomfortable | warm

positive	neutral	negative

b) Analyse the atmosphere in one of the parts of the story listed in task 5.

Tips The setting often plays an important role in shaping the atmosphere in a story. As do the characters and how they act, and the narrative perspective. Often it is useful to pay special attention to the adjectives and adverbs used.

12 CHOOSE

In Ms. Anita's car Ellery's parents confront their daughter with her behaviour. Based on what you have learnt about the characters in the story write a conversation between her parents, Ellery, and Ms. Anita.

OR

A couple of days after the competition, Ellery comes over to Ms. Anita's place to practice the piano. Ms. Anita right away realizes that something is wrong with Ellery. She tells her about the day of the competition and how she felt about Lori's behaviour. Write the dialogue.

Checklist

Doing a creative task

✓ Have I used the same style and the same words the character would use?
✓ Is the way he or she acts or speaks according to the way he or she has behaved at other times in the story?
✓ Is what I am writing realistic?

Metaphors

13

The cicadas are often mentioned in the story.

a) Mark the passages, where the cicadas are mentioned or referred to.

b) Obviously, they have a metaphoric meaning. Analyse these lines and interpret what this meaning could be.

Author and oeuvre

14

a) Read the extracts from some reviews on author Camille Acker's short story collection *Training school for negro girls* (2018).

> "The lives of the girls and women featured in these stories are rendered with tremendous warmth, humor, and care. Camille Acker has written pages that are saturated with the stuff of black life in Washington, DC: the cadences, the music, the aspirations, the trouble, the disappointments, the inventiveness, and the laughter. *Training School for Negro Girls* is a wonderful debut."

> "These stories pulse with vitality as ordinary people look for a future in a world that doesn't expect them to have one... A striking cross-section view of the capital's corners, these stories contain, and sometimes restrain, hope; in fleeting glimpses, they also reveal the beginning of a way out."

b) **Pair work** Choose a quote and explain to your partner to what extent the reviews above are true for "Cicada".

Fatima, the Biloquist: A Transformation Story (2018)

PRE-READING

1

Looking at the title, what would you guess the story could be about?

biloquist – A biloquist is someone who has the ability to speak in two different voices.

How to deal with unknown words

2

In the story you will come across some words that you might not know. To avoid frustration and looking up every unknown word in a dictionary, the following guideline can help you understand the text.

① **Find** the unknown word.

② **Mark** the unknown word.

③ **Decide:** Is ist important to understand the text?

not important: I can do without!	important: I need to find out the meaning.

④ a) Can I get the meaning from the **context**?
b) Are there similar words in German, French or Latin?
c) Is there a similar word in English that I know (word family: verb / adjective / noun etc.)?

I understand the meaning.	I still don't understand it.
	⑤ Look it up in the dictionary.

⑥ **Write** the word and the translation down (in your vocabulary book, on an index card or above the word in the short story).

a) Write down which of the steps has helped you to understand the words below.
b) Then write down the German translation.
c) Pick another five words that are unknown to you and find their meaning with the help of the guideline.
Examples from pp. 72-73:
Condensation (l. 10) – step 4 b: "condensation" is similar to the German word *Kondensation*
Meaning and translation: condensation consists of small drops of water which form when warm water vapour or steam touches a cold surface such as a window. German: *Kondensation*
blended (l. 14) – infinitive: "to blend" – step 3: The word is not directly needed to understand the text. Or step 4 c: A blended whiskey is a whiskey that is mixed from different sorts or batches. German: *mischen*

1. recited (l. 12) – ______________________
2. freckles (l. 27) – ______________________
3. rolled her eyes (at so) (l. 32) – ______________________
4. encountered (l. 53) – ______________________
5. to be dropped off / to drop off (l. 55) – ______________________
6. sauntered up (l. 69) – ______________________

Research on popular culture mentioned in the story

3

Throughout the story you will be confronted with elements of popular culture of the 1990s.

Group work

a) Note down who or what you can see in the pictures. You can find tips in the box below.
b) Categorize the words from the box and write them into the table below.
c) Mark everything considered being part of "the white culture" in green – if you cannot find out, do not mark it.

No Limit • Master P • FUBU shirts • Jordans • Silverchair • Rick James • Kastels • Yo! MTV Raps • The Parkers • Countess Vaughn • Wild Things • Denise Richards • Cash Money • Bad Boy • Wu-Tang • Boyz II Men • ABC • BBD • ODB • LDB • TLC • B-I-G-P-O-P-P-A • The Smiths • Morrissey • Rush Hour • Beamer • Taurus • Countee Cullen • Baratunde Thurston • Ralph Ellison • Steve Martin • Jennifer Beals • Montclair Plaza • Upland • Hillwood • Dickies • Patti Mayonnaise • Doug (Funnie) • The Fresh Prince of Bel Air • Will • Ashley Banks

places	brands	musicians

actors and actresses	films / TV shows	other

Fatima, The Biloquist[1]: A Transformation Story

by Nafissa Thompson-Spires

There are happier stories one could tell about Fatima. In the nineties you could be whatever you wanted – someone said that on the news – and by 1998 Fatima felt ready to become black, full black, baa baa black sheep black, black like the elbows and knees on praying folk black, if only someone would teach her.

Up to that point she had existed like a sort of colorless gas, or a bit of moisture[2], leaving the residue[3] of something familiar, sweat stains[4] on a T-shirt, hot breath on the back of a neck, condensation rings on wood, but never a fullness of whatever matter had formed them.

The week she met Violet, Fatima had recited[5] "An Address to the Ladies, by their Best Friend Sincerity[6]" before her eleventh grade AP English class[7]. She blended her makeup to perfection that morning, but the other students barely looked at her, instead busying themselves by clicking and replacing the lead in mechanical pencils or folding and flicking paper footballs over finger goal posts – even during the part she recited with the most emphasis: "Ah! sad, perverse, degenerate[8] race / The monstrous head deforms the face." They clapped dull palms for a few seconds as Fatima sulked[9] back to her desk. But they sat up, alert, when Wally "The Wigger[10]" Arnett recited "Incident[11]" and said the word that always made the white kids pay attention.

"You know, I identify with Countee Cullen[12] and all," Wally, with brown freckles[13] and a floppy brown haircut, finished up. "He was a black man, and he was, like, oppressed[14] for who he was and stuff."

The hands pounded a hero's applause as Wally headed back to his seat next to Fatima looking like he expected a high five. She rolled her eyes at him, but she couldn't articulate her wrath[15] into something more specific. Later that morning, when Wally asked her for the fourth time that semester whether she listened to No Limit rappers, she lunged at[16] his face. She had previously tried to explain to Wally, in so many words and dirty looks, that he was not and could not become an honorary black man through his love of Master P. He wore a vague smile that Fatima sometimes read as smug and sometimes as vapid[17], but he never seemed to hear her. He who would not hear, however, would feel – or would have if Mrs. Bishop hadn't sent Fatima to the principal to "cool down" before her fingernails could scratch off any of Wally's freckles.

It wasn't fair, Fatima thought, that Wally was praised, even mildly popular, for his FUBU shirts and Jordans with the tags still on them, yet Fatima was called "ghetto supastar" the one time she outlined her lips with dark pencil. Nor was it fair that she should get a warning from Principal Lee for "looking like she might become violent" when Wally said "nigger" and got applause. She was still thinking about Wally when she first encountered Violet. They met at the Montclair Plaza, where Fatima had been dropped off by her mother, Monica, along with the warnings that she better not (1) exceed[18] her allowance[19]

Annotations

1 **biloquist** = sb who can speak in two different voices
2 **moisture** = a moderate degree of wetness
3 **residue** = this remains after sth else has been removed
4 **stain** = a dirty mark
5 to **recite** = to repeat aloud before an audience
6 **"An Address to the Ladies, by their Best Friend Sincerity"** = poem by Charles Brockden Brown (1771-1810)
7 **AP English class** = short for Advanced Placement; a course at high school for advanced pupils, who can skip the first year of college when they have passed the final exam
8 **degenerate** = having lost all good qualities
9 to **sulk** = to look angry because you are upset
10 **wigger** = slang word for a white person who wants to be part of the African American community and spends time learning about this culture
11 **"Incident"** = a 1920 poem by Countee Cullen about his experience of being called the N-word at age eight by a white boy of a similar age.
12 **Countee Cullen** = The text includes a number of names of writers, bands, singers etc. which are especially marked.
13 **freckle** = a small spot usually on the face caused by the sun
14 to **be oppressed** = to be mistreated
15 **wrath** = great anger
16 to **lunge at** = to make a move toward a person in order to hurt him / her
17 **vapid** = to be obsessed with oneself
18 to **exceed** = to go beyond a certain limit
19 **allowance** = pocket money

of fifty dollars; (2) use her emergency credit card for nonemergencies; or (3) pick up any riffraff[20], roughnecks[21], or pregnancies while she was there. Number three was highly unlikely, and Fatima knew Monica knew it, but she said it anyway.

Fatima moped[22] near the Clinique counter with her heavy Discman tucked in a tiny backpack and her headphones wrapped around her neck, trying to decide between one shade of lipstick and another. The college student behind the counter ignored her, chatting with another colleague, and in situations like this, Fatima usually bought something expensive just to show the salesperson that she could. A blond girl with a short bob[23] sauntered[24] up next to her and said, "The burgundy is pretty, but you could do something darker."

Fatima peripherally[25] saw the hair first, so she didn't expect the rest of the package. A voluptuous[26] – really, that was the only word that would work – girl with a wide nose and black features stood next to her. Fatima had a friend with albinism[27] before in preschool[28] who wore thick red glasses and had blushed almost the same color when she wet her pants at naptime once. She recognized in Violet similar features.

"But you could get the same stuff at Claire's for cheaper," Violet said. "It's not like old girl's trying to help you anyway."

The salesgirl, not chastened[29] but amused, moved back to her post and said, "May I help you," in one of those voices that mean "Get lost."

"I'm still – " Fatima started.

But the blond black girl spoke again: "We'd like some free samples[30] of some of the lipsticks, that color"– she pointed, reaching over Fatima to a pot of dark gloss – "and that one."

"We only give samples," the salesgirl said, "to – "

"To everyone who asks, right?" Violet finished.

The sales associate frowned, looked back at her colleague, looked at Violet and Fatima, and frowned again. "I'll get those ready for you," she said.

Fatima considered putting her headphones back on and trying to float out[31] of the department store, away from this loud girl with the jarring[32] features and booming voice.

"Here," Violet said, handing her the dark gloss in its tiny gloss pot.

"You keep it," Fatima said and started trying to vaporize[33] toward the shoe department.

"It's for you," the girl said, following her.

And like that, they were friends, or something to that effect.

It was Violet's appraisal[34] – "You're, like, totally a white girl, aren't you?" – that set Fatima into motion. They were eating dots of ice cream that same day at the food court after Violet showed Fatima how to get samples from Estee Lauder, Elizabeth Arden, and MAC. Fatima felt a little like a gangster, holding up the reluctant salesgirls for their stash[35], but she had a nearly full bag of swag[36] by then, perfume, lip gloss, and oil-blotting papers, without spending any of her allowance. It was already too good to be true, so she didn't feel sad when Violet said "white girl," but almost relieved by the inevitable[37].

Fatima had been accused of whiteness and being a traitor to the race before, whenever she spoke up in Sunday school at her AME church[38] or visited her family in Southeast San Diego (South east a universal geographical marker for the ghetto) or when a cute guy who was just about to ask her out backed away, saying, "You go to private school, don't you?" It was why she didn't have any black friends – and why, she worried, she would never have a boyfriend, even riffraff to upset her mother. The allegations[39] offended her but never moved her to any action other than private crying or retreating further into her melancholy belief that her school, Westwood Prep[40], and her parents' high-paying jobs, had made her somehow unfit for black people. Rather than respond, she usually turned up her Discman louder, sinking into the distantly black but presently white sounds of ska and punk, and sang under her breath, "I'm a freak / I'm a freak" (in the style of Silverchair, not Rick James). At the moment she especially enjoyed reading Charles Brockden Brown and daydreaming of a sickly boyfriend like Arthur Mervyn[41]. If black people wouldn't accept her, she would stick to what she knew.

But Violet's judgment held more heft[42], in her critique a possibility for transformation. When a black girl with natural green eyes and blond hair and a big chest and bubble butt[43] tells you that you, with your sable skin and dark hair, are not black enough, you listen.

[20] **riffraff** = not well-educated people
[21] **roughneck** = impolite person
[22] to **mope** = to do nothing, feeling sorry for yourself
[23] **bob** = a haircut
[24] to **saunter** = to go slowly and in a relaxed way
[25] **peripherally** = in passing
[26] **voluptuous** = sexy
[27] **albinism** = having white hair and skin
[28] **preschool** = early childhood education before primary school
[29] to **be chastened** = to make sb feel sorry for what he / she has done
[30] **(free) sample** = a small piece of a product given to try it out
[31] to **float out** = to move in an easy way
[32] **jarring** = to be noticeable in a negative way

[33] to **vaporize** = here: to disappear
[34] **appraisal** = judgement
[35] **stash** = reserve
[36] **swag** = sth that has been stolen
[37] **inevitable** = impossible to avoid
[38] **AME church** = short for African Methodist Episcopal Church: a Christian church with mostly African American members
[39] **allegation** = accusation which must not be based on facts
[40] **Westwood Prep** = private school which prepares pupils for entry exams
[41] **Arthur Mervyn** = protagonist of one of Charles Brockden Brown's more popular novels: a farm boy who moves to Philadelphia and becomes a man of urban, eighteenth century America. He acts according to his convictions but is at the same time also a very analytical person. In the end he marries the first Jewish-American character in American fiction.
[42] **heft** = weight
[43] **butt** = short for buttock (*slang*); you sit on your bottom

"It's not that I'm trying to be white. It's just that's what I'm around."

"You don't have no church friends? You adopted? Your parents white, too?" Violet didn't seem to want a response. "Where do you stay?"

"With my parents." Fatima wondered if something was wrong with Violet for asking such a stupid question.

"I mean where do you live?" Violet asked.

"Upland."

"They got black people there. My cousin Frankie lives there," Violet said, chewing the dots of ice cream in a way that set Fatima's teeth on edge. She wore a tight white top, cream Dickies, and white Adidas tennis shoes.

"Yes, but not on my street." Fatima wore a pink cardigan, black Dickies, and skater shoes, Kastels.

Violet paused her crunching and talking for a moment. "You have a boyfriend?"

Fatima shook her head. "Do you?"

"I'm in between options right now. Anyway, the last one is locked up in Tehachapi.[44]"

Fatima nodded. She had a cousin who had served time[45] there. He called her bourgie[46], and she'd kicked him in the face once, delighting in his fat lip and his inability to hit girls.

"I'm kidding," Violet said. "We don't all get locked up."

Fatima stuttered.

"I can see I'ma have to teach you a lot of things. You ready?" Violet meant ready to leave the food court, but Fatima meant more when she said, "Yeah, I'm ready." And thus began her transformation.

If only Baratunde Thurston had been writing when Fatima came of age[47], she could have learned how to be black from a book instead of from Violet's charm school. Even a quick glance at Ralph Ellison could have saved her a lot of trouble, but she wasn't ready for that, caught up, as she was, in the dramas of Arthur Mervyn and Carwin[48], the Biloquist, and all of them. With Violet's help, Fatima absorbed the sociocultural knowledge she'd missed – not through osmosis or through more relevant literature, but through committed, structured ethnographical study[49]. She immersed[50] herself in slang as rigorously[51] as she would later immerse herself in Spanish for her foreign-language exam in grad school[52]; she pored over *Vibe* magazine and watched *Yo! MTV Raps* and *The Parkers*, trying to work her mouth around phrases with the same intonation that Countess Vaughn used, a sort of combination of a Jersey accent and a speech impediment[53]. When she couldn't get into those texts, she encouraged herself with the old episodes of *Fresh Prince of Bel-Air* that played in constant early-morning and late-night rotation, feeling assured that if Ashley Banks could, after five seasons, become almost as cool as Will, then she could, too. Her new turns of phrase[54] fit her about as awkwardly as the puffy powder-blue FUBU jacket she found in a thrift[55] store in downtown Rialto.

Still, she was happy when Violet looked approvingly at it. Pale Violet became the arbiter[56] of Fatima's blackness, the purveyor[57] of all things authentic. Though she was five feet eight and chunky[58] by most standards – nearly obese by Fatima's – you would think Violet, judging by the way she walked, was Pamela Anderson, like a hula doll[59] on a dashboard swinging hips and breasts.

The distance between their respective houses was fifteen minutes, but only seven if they met halfway, Fatima borrowing her father's extra car (the 1993 Beamer, so as not to look ostentatious[60]) and Violet getting a ride from one of her brothers or occasionally driving her mother's old Taurus. They never met at each other's houses, lest[61] Fatima's upper-middle opulence embarrass Violet, and because there was no space for Violet to carve out for herself at her house.

Violet made Fatima a study guide of the top ten black expressions for rating attractive men, and they practiced the pronunciations together. The pinnacle[62] of hotness, according to Violet, was either "dangfoine[63]," "hella foine[64]," or "bout it, bout it[65]," as in "Oooh, he bout it, bout it." This phrase especially required the Countess Vaughn intonation and often included spontaneous bouts[66] of raising the roof[67].

During their tutoring sessions, Fatima stifled[68] her joke about the rain in Spain falling mostly on the plains and practiced on, assured that Violet's instruction would confer upon[69] her, like Carwin, "a wonderful gift" of biloquism.

[44] **Tehachapi** = an American small city with a high percentage of prisoners
[45] to **serve time** = to spend time in a prison
[46] **bourgie** = (*slang*) sb who supports traditional values (*Spießbürger*)
[47] to **come of age** = Adolescents come of age in Germany at the age of 18.
[48] **Carwin** = protagonist of *Memoirs of Carwin the biloquist* by Charles Brockden Brown about a farmer boy who wants to have a good education which his father denies him. He obtains the power to impersonate different people and uses it to achieve his goals.
[49] **ethnographical study** = The aim is to gain an understanding of a social or cultural group.
[50] to **immerse oneself in** = to be completely involved in sth
[51] **rigorously** = intensely
[52] **grad school** = university to get a master degree

[53] **speech impediment** = having problems that make it difficult to speak in a normal way
[54] **turn of phrase** = way of expressing oneself
[55] **thrift** = non-profit second hand shop
[56] **arbiter** = a person who has the power to decide what will be done
[57] **purveyor** = sb who supplies sth (e.g. a product)
[58] **chunky / obese** = heavy, fat
[59] **hula doll** = *Puppe im Bastrock*
[60] **ostentatious** = to be boastful
[61] **lest** = unless
[62] **pinnacle** = the high point
[63] **dangfoine** = really attractive
[64] **hella foine** = really attractive
[65] **bout it, bout it** = originally a way to say you are open to try sth new from a song by Master P called "bout it, bout it", and changed to mean sb very attractive
[66] **bout** = short attack
[67] to **raise the roof** = a dance move where a person raises their arms above their head and back down multiple times
[68] to **stifle** = to prevent from happening; to suppress
[69] to **confer upon sb** = to give sb sth

Glossaries[70] soon followed, in which Violet broke down slang that had previously mystified Fatima. She couldn't wait to replace her traditional "fer shure" with "fisshow" in a real conversation, but she took issue with[71] some of Violet's recommendations, especially "nigga" and "gangsta," which Violet explained as terms of endearment[72]. "So basically," Fatima summarized, ventriloquizing[73] Ashley Banks again, "you want me to turn good things into bad things and vice versa."

Violet said, "Mostly."

Fatima tried pumping her shoulders in a brief Bankhead Bounce[74], but it was obvious she lacked the follow-through and wasn't ready for dancing yet.

And it was almost like any romantic comedy in which the sassy[75] black person moves in with the white people and teaches them how to live their lives in color and put some bass in their voices, only Steve Martin wasn't in it, and no one was a maid or a butler or nanny, and the romance was between two girls, and it was platonic[76], and they were both black this time, but one didn't look like it, and one didn't sound like it, at least not consistently[77].

"They racist up[78] at that school? I can't stand cocky[79] white people," Violet said one day while they sat at their usual table, near the flower divider in the mall's arboretum[80]. Some white guys from Hillwood sat across the way, laughing loudly.

Fatima didn't like to talk about her school, but everyone in the Inland Empire[81] knew Westwood and Hillwood, rivals on and off the football field. "I don't think so," Fatima said.

"What do you mean you don't think so? Either something's racist or it's not."

No one at school poked out[82] his tongue and called her that, like they did in the poem Wally read, but Fatima thought about Wally, his affectations[83], and Principal Lee. "It's not always comfortable," she said. "It can be awkward, but I'm awkward."

"You sure are." Violet laughed, and Fatima laughed, too. She was learning to do more of that, and to wear a kind of selfassuredness with her side-swooped Aaliyah bangs[84]. In fact, most interactions were easier with Violet than they were with others. Violet understood things. Fatima never had to explain why she might wrap her hair in a silk scarf at bedtime or why she always carried a tube of hand cream to prevent not only chapped[85] hands, but also allover ashiness[86]. Those shared practices validated[87] Fatima, and so did Violet's understanding of Fatima's fears about her body. "Sometimes I just feel horrible about all of it, the sweating, the bleeding. I don't always feel like a regular girl, you know?" Fatima said one day, "But what is normal anyway?"

"Word, that's deep[88]," Violet said, and explained that she, too, felt the weight of her body, because it did not look "like what people expect black to be." In spite of her seeming confidence, Violet confided, she had a complex about her albinism. Fatima understood when Violet intimated[89] that albinism marked her as both desirable for her lightness[90], her hair color, her eye color, and yet despised for some perceived physical untruth. Fatima had seen the way people glanced two and three times at Violet, deciding where to place her and whether she warranted[91] any of the benefits of whiteness. Violet could call other black people like Fatima white, but to be called white herself pushed Violet to violent tears. Just ask her ex-boyfriend and her ex-friend Kandice from middle school, who had called her Patti Mayonnaise in a fit of anger and gotten a beat down that made her wet her pants like Fatima's preschool friend.

"Why Patti Mayonnaise?" Fatima said.

"You know, from Doug, she was the black girl on the DL[92] who looked white, and mayonnaise is white. It's a stupid joke."

"Patti was black?" Fatima said.

"Girl, a whole lot of everybody got black in them," Violet started.

Fatima had heard some of Violet's theories before during a game they sometimes played on the phone. The list included Jennifer Beals, Mariah Carey, and "that freaky girl from *Wild Things*" Denise Richards, and now, apparently, Patti Mayonnaise. When Fatima suggested Justin Timberlake, Violet said, "Nah, he's like that Wally kid at your school."

The nuances of these and other things Emily, Fatima's best friend since second grade, just couldn't understand, no matter how earnestly she tried or how many questions she asked, like why they couldn't share shampoo when she slept over, or "What does 'For us, by us'[93] even mean," and why Fatima's top lip was darker than her bottom one.

[70] **glossary** = a list of special words which are explained
[71] to **take issue with sb** = to disagree with
[72] **terms of endearment** = words which show that you like sb a lot
[73] to **ventriloquize** = to talk with different voices as if you were a different person
[74] **Bankhead Bounce** = a dance that originated in a neighbourhood on the west side of Atlanta known as Bankheadd; It is performed by moving one's shoulders up and down with arms bent toward the chest.
[75] **sassy** = sb who doesn't follow rules
[76] **platonic** = not involving sex
[77] **consistently** = always
[78] to **racist up** = (*slang*) to become more and more racist
[79] **cocky** = sb who thinks he / she is better than anyone else
[80] **arboretum** = garden with trees
[81] **Inland Empire** = a college in Upland
[82] to **poke out one's tongue** = to show one's tongue
[83] **affectation** = pretence
[84] **side-swooped Aaliyah bangs** = popular hairstyle which goes back to Aaliyah who was a popular American R & B singer
[85] **chapped** = rough
[86] **ashiness** = here: dry skin
[87] to **validate** = to approve of
[88] **that's deep** = a turn of phrase often used by people to comment on a point giving lots of insight or being philosophical
[89] to **intimate** = to frighten sb so they do what you want
[90] **lightness** = relative whiteness
[91] to **warrant** = to justify
[92] **DL** = short for 'on the down low' which is when a piece of information is hidden on purpose, or is not widely known
[93] **'For us, by us'** = short form is FUBU; an American hip hop clothing company

Fatima picked up some theories on her own, too, without Violet or the literature. The thing about the brown top lip and the pink lower one, Fatima had pieced together after what she learned from Violet and what she had learned at school, was that you could either read them as two souls trying to merge[94] into a better self, or you could conceal them under makeup and talk with whichever lip was convenient for the occasion. At school and with Emily, she talked with her pink lip, and with Violet, she talked with her brown one, and that created tension only if she thought too much about it.

Fatima passed the time at school by imagining the time she would spend after school with Violet, who promised to teach her how to flirt better on their next excursion and to possibly, eventually, hook her up[95] with one of her cousins, but not one of her brothers, because "Most of them aren't good for anything except upsetting your mother, if you want to do that." Fatima did not want to do that.

Now at school when Wally the Wigger looked like he was even thinking about saying something to her, Fatima made a face that warned, "Don't even look like you're thinking about saying something to me," and he obeyed. In her mind, she not only said this aloud, but said it in Violet's voice.

She didn't mind the laughter in her parents' eyes when she tried out a new phrase or hairstyle, because it was all working. There was something prettier about her now, too, and people seemed to see it before Fatima did, because a guy named Rolf at Westwood — a tall brunette in her history class, with whom she'd exchanged a few eye rolls over Wally — asked her for her phone number. Without pausing to consider anything, she gave it to him.

IT MIGHT SEEM, up to this point, that Fatima simultaneously wore braces[96], glasses, and forehead acne, when you hardly needed to glance to see the gloss of her black hair or the sheen[97] on her shins[98], with or without lotion. Fatima knew this truth instinctively, but buried its warmth under the shame of early-childhood teasing[99] and a preference for melancholy self-pity. It was more romantic to feel ugly than to pretend she couldn't hold her head just right, unleash[100] her beautiful teeth, and make a skeptical man kneel at her skirt's hem[101]. She just didn't have the practice, but she was hopeful that she might get it, with Rolf or one of Violet's cousins, hopeful that the transformation had taken hold.

[94] to **merge** = to combine
[95] to **hook sb up with sb else** = to match them together as a couple
[96] **braces** = you wear them to hold your teeth in position
[97] **sheen** = the shine
[98] **shin** = front part of the leg below the knee
[99] to **tease** = to make fun of sb
[100] to **unleash** = to release
[101] **hem** = the edge of a piece of clothing

She had just returned from a movie with Violet — where not one but two guys had asked for her phone number, though three had asked for Violet's, pronouncing their approval of her "thickness" with grunts[102], smiles, and by looking directly at her butt — when her mother said, "You got a phone call, from a boy."

It couldn't be one of the boys from the theater already; that would make anyone look desperate.

"Who is Rolf?" her mother asked with a smile, "and why didn't you mention him before?"

Fatima nearly floated up to her bedroom. She thought about calling Violet but called Rolf back instead, waiting, of course, for an hour to pass, a tip she had learned from Violet in the event of a hypothetical situation such as this.

By now, and with some authenticity, Fatima could intone[103] the accent marks in places they hadn't been before, recite all the names of all the members of Cash Money, Bad Boy, No Limit, Wu-Tang, Boyz II Men, ABC, BBD, ODB, LDB, TLC, B-I-G-P-O-P-P-A, Ronny, Bobby, Ricky, Mike, Ralph, Johnny, Tony, Toni, and Tone, if she wanted. But when she called Rolf, all they talked about were skateboards and the Smiths, in whose music Fatima had dabbled[104] before Violet.

"The Smiths are way better than Morrissey," Rolf said. His voice was nasal but deep.

"You can barely tell the difference since Morrissey's voice is so overpowering," she said, from her pink lip.

"No, but the Smiths' stuff is way darker," Rolf said. "You should hear the first album. Then you'll get it. I've got it on vinyl."

"Okay," Fatima waited.

She noticed that he didn't invite her over to listen or offer to lend her the album, but he did call back two days later and ask if she wanted to hang out over the next weekend, "like at the mall or something, see a movie?"

Fatima counted to twelve, as per the rules (the universal ones, not just Violet's) and said, "Yeah, that'd be cool." She almost left the "l" off the end of the word, but caught herself. "Which mall?"

"Where else?" Rolf said. "The Montclair Plaza."

This would be her first date, and though that was the kind of thing to share with a best friend, especially one with more experience, Fatima felt— in some deep way that hurt her stomach— that Violet didn't need to know about Rolf, not yet at least. She would keep her lips glossed and parted, her two worlds separate.

The week leading up to the first date, Fatima tried to play extra-cool, asking Violet more questions than usual when they spoke on the phone. Neither of the guys from the movie theatre had called Fatima, but one of Violet's three

[102] **grunt** = a short sound to show disapproval
[103] to **intone** = to say sth without much expression
[104] to **dabble** = to have an interest but in a superficial way

had asked Violet out, and she was "letting him stew[105] for a while before I let him know. Anyway, I thought you wanted to check out *Rush Hour* this weekend."

"This weekend?" Fatima said.

"This weekend."

"I told my parents I would babysit this weekend, I forgot," Fatima lied, feeling a bit like a grease[106] stain on a silk shirt.

"Since when?" Violet pushed.

"We can go next weekend, or during the week," Fatima said, and changed the subject.

Before they got off the phone, Violet said, "I guess I'll call Mike back, then, and tell him I'm free after all."

Fatima would say that she wasn't embarrassed by Violet or Rolf, but she wasn't ready for them to meet. She felt relief, then, when their first and second dates went without a hitch[107] — and ended with a gentle but sort of indifferent kiss — and even more relieved that Rolf was okay with seeing each other during the week so that Fatima wouldn't have to explain to Violet why she suddenly had other plans on Friday and Saturday evenings.

"Tell me more about your other friends," Rolf had said on the phone one night, when Fatima was starting to think she might love him. He knew Emily from school. He knew she went to an AME church.

He'd met her parents and siblings by then, though she still hadn't met his. When he first came over to the house, he shook hands with Fatima's father — noting Mr. Willis's height with a "Whoa, you're tall" — and hugged her mother and patted her six-year-old brother's head awkwardly, in a way that reminded Fatima of someone stroking a rabbit's foot for luck.

At dinner Rolf chatted to excess, complimenting the drapes, the silverware, and Fatima's frowny-faced eight-year-old sister and indifferent younger brother. She wasn't sure how nervous either of them should be. She found his foot with hers under the table and smiled silently, "Calm down. Be quiet." She tried to signal, but Rolf prattled[108] on, "I think it's great that you as a black family are so successful."

No one addressed Rolf, but her parents stood to clear the dishes. She heard their irritation in faint whispers from the kitchen, could see it in their eyes even with their backs turned. Fatima declined dessert. "We have to get to the movies. We'll get some candy there," she said.

Still, she and Rolf were together a month later, and her parents hadn't expressed any concrete disapproval. A month later, she was only just telling Rolf about Violet.

"I guess my other best friend," Fatima responded, "besides Emily, is Violet."

"Violet," Rolf repeated. "Cool name. She's not at Westwood, is she?"

"No, public school."

"Ah," Rolf said, in a tone that Fatima interpreted as neutral.

"She's my girl." She stopped herself from saying "Ace boon coon[109]." "We hang out a lot on the weekends, actually."

"How come you never mentioned her before?"

"I don't know." Fatima felt her mouth lying again, moving somehow separately from her real voice. "She's kind of shy. She got teased a lot."

"Oh, that's too bad," Rolf said.

"They called her Patti Mayonnaise," Fatima said, and she didn't know why it was she who was now prattling on.

"Don't tell anybody this, but I always thought Patty was cute on Doug," Rolf said, and shifted to talking about all his favourite cartoons. Fatima exhaled.

Over time they grew to joke, a little awkwardly, about Fatima's position at school, as one of two black girls. She asked Rolf if this was a thing for him or if she was his first black girlfriend, because by now they called each other boyfriend and girlfriend.

"I don't see color," he said. "I just saw you. Like, one day there you were."

Violet would have said that color-blind people were the same ones who followed you in the store and that Rolf's game was hella corny[110].

"Anyway, it's not like you're black black," Rolf said.

Fatima remembered the lifelessness, before Violet, of feeling like a colorless gas and tried, in spite of a dull ache and the numbness of her brown lip, to take Rolf's words as a compliment.

The conventions of such a transformation dictate that a snuggletooth[111] or broken heel threatens to return the heroine to her former life. That snaggletooth, for Fatima, was either Rolf or Violet, depending on how you looked at things, and Fatima wasn't sure how she did.

When she saw Violet, on April 4 — after hiding her relationship with Rolf for three months — approaching from across the lobby of Edwards Cinema with Mike's arm around her waist, Fatima's first instinct was to grab Rolf's hand and steer him toward the exit. But Violet was already calling her name.

This wasn't the natural order of things, for these separate lives to converge[112]. Other factors aside, the code went hos before bros[113], school life before social life, family before anyone else. But Rolf was both school and social,

[105] to **let sb stew** = to let sb wait before he / she gets an answer
[106] **grease** = animal fat
[107] **hitch** = problem
[108] to **prattle** = to go on talking without a pause

[109] **ace boon coon** = a very good friend
[110] to **be corny** = lacking originality
[111] **snaggletooth** = a broken or irregularly standing tooth
[112] to **converge** = to get closer and closer
[113] **hos before bros** = normally the other way round: "bros before hoes"; (*slang*) which refers to a male placing more importance on his male friend group than a girlfriend

and Violet both social and nearly family, and Fatima's math skills couldn't balance this equation.

"I knew I saw you," Violet said to Fatima once she got close. "Who is this?"

"Rolf, Violet. Violet, Rolf," Fatima said, "and Mike."

Mike smiled, and Rolf smiled, and they shook hands, but neither young woman saw the guys, their eyes deadlocked[114] on each other.

"Ha, so this is Violet," Rolf said, ignoring or misreading Fatima's firm grip on his arm. "Even your black friends are white, too." Rolf laughed.

"I was gonna tell you — " Fatima started to say to Violet.

"Wait, Patti Mayonnaise, I get it now," Rolf said aloud, then, "Oops, I — " and both women scowled at[115] him.

Fatima made a noise that could be interpreted as either a guffaw[116] or a deep moan[117].

When she turned back to Violet, though she opened and closed her mouth several times, no sounds emerged. She didn't mean to hurt her; some things had just come out, and other things she hadn't told Violet because she wasn't sure which lip she was supposed to use. Before she knew it, her voice was over there and then over there, and she was ventriloquizing what she'd learned all at once, but from too many places and all at the wrong time. Violet didn't curse[118] or buck up[119] as though she might hit Fatima — though perhaps one of those options might have been better; she just grabbed Mike's arm and walked away.

And like that, Fatima was a vapor again, but something darker, like a funnel cloud[120], or black smoke that mocked what was already singed[121].

[114] to **deadlock** = unable to move
[115] to **scowl at sb** = to make an angry frown
[116] **guffaw** = a loud laugh
[117] **moan** = a low cry
[118] to **curse** = to swear
[119] to **buck up** = to gather up all one's courage
[120] **funnel cloud** = *Rauchwolke*
[121] **singed** = to have a burnt surface

WHILE READING

Reading strategies

4

Depending on what you actually want from a text or what task you have to solve, there are different reading strategies. Reciprocal reading that can improve your comprehension can consist of the following parts: *clarifying, asking questions, summarizing, anticipating* and *giving a possible heading*. For example:

There are happier stories one could tell about Fatima. In the nineties you could be whatever you wanted — someone said that on the news — and by 1998 Fatima felt ready to become black, full black, baa baa black sheep black, black like the elbows and knees on praying folk black, if only someone would teach her.	1 **clarifying**: First the reader should clarify whether he or she has understood the text. *Basically everything is understandable, but it is not clear what "baa baa black sheep black" means. Also it is not clear what the elbows and knees of praying people means. It may become clear after having read more.* 2 **asking questions**. What questions derive from what you have read? *Why isn't the story happy?* *What kind of person is Fatima? Is she religious?* 3 **summarizing**: What have I just read? *The text deals with Fatima who in 1998 would like to have someone teach her how to be black. Obviously the story is not a happy one.* 4 **anticipating**: How could the story continue? *Probably she will find someone who teaches her. Maybe this won't make her happy.* 5 **giving a possible heading**: *Fatima wanting to explore her black identitiy*

It is helpful to underline parts of the text, highlight passages and write next to the text, following the strategy above.

Group work (5)

a) Practice that with the next parts of the story. Decide who does 1, 2 etc.

b) After each part present / discuss your findings and questions with your group.

Up to that point she had existed like a sort of colorless gas, or a bit of moisture[1], leaving the residue[2] of something familiar, sweat stains[3] on a T-shirt, hot breath on the back of a neck, condensation rings on wood, but never a fullness of whatever matter had formed them. **Annotations** [1] **moisture** = a moderate degree of wetness [2] **residue** = this remains after sth else has been removed [3] **stain** = a dirty mark	**1 clarifying:** **2 asking questions:** **3 summarizing:** **4 anticipating:** **5 giving a possible heading:**
The week she met Violet, Fatima had recited[1] "An Address to the Ladies, by their Best Friend Sincerity[2]" before her eleventh grade AP English class[3]. She blended her makeup to perfection that morning, but the other students barely looked at her, instead busying themselves by clicking and replacing the lead in mechanical pencils or folding and flicking paper footballs over finger goal posts — even during the part she recited with the most emphasis: "Ah! sad, perverse, degenerate[4] race / The monstrous head deforms the face." They clapped dull palms for a few seconds as Fatima sulked[5] back	**1 clarifying:** **2 asking questions:** **3 summarizing:**

Annotations

[1] to **recite** = to repeat aloud before an audience

[2] **"An Address to the Ladies, by their Best Friend Sincerity"** = poem by Charles Brockden Brown (1771-1810)

[3] **AP English class** = short for Advanced Placement; a course at high school for advanced pupils, who can skip the first year of college when they have passed the final exam

[4] **degenerate** = having lost all good qualities

[5] to **sulk** = to look angry because you are upset

to her desk. But they sat up, alert, when Wally "The Wigger[6]" Arnett recited "Incident[7]" and said the word that always made the white kids pay attention. "You know, I identify with Countee Cullen and all," Wally, with brown freckles[8] and a floppy brown haircut, finished up. "He was a black man, and he was, like, oppressed[9] for who he was and stuff."	**4 anticipating:** **5 giving a possible heading:**

Annotations

[6] **wigger** = slang word for a white person who feels part of the African American community and spends time learning about this culture

[7] **"Incident"** = a 1920 poem by Countee Cullen about his experience of being called the N-word at age eight by a white boy of a similar age.

[8] **freckle** = a small spot usually on the face caused by the sun

[9] to **be oppressed** = to be mistreated

LISTENING

5 Webcode DSW-73685-09

In a video-podcast called Literary Roadhouse the three hosts Anais, Gerald and Andy discuss the short story. Listen to an extract from the video-podcast (02:08-04:46). → **S12** How to listen / watch effectively

a) Complete the sentences.

b) **Pair work** Compare with a partner. Then add and / or change answers.

1. Anais summarizes the plot of the story. Gerald says the story has ____________ words.
2. Anais sums up that Fatima goes ____________
3. At her school Fatima is ____________ but not ____________
4. Violet teaches Fatima how to ____________, ____________, and ____________
5. Fatima realizes she is codeswitching which means that ____________
6. Fatima doesn't want to tell Violet about Rolf as she somewhat feels that ____________
7. Violet is sensitive because she was ____________
8. After the meeting at the cinema Fatima feels ____________

POST-READING

6 **Pair work**

a) Divide the story into meaningful paragraphs.

b) Give them headings.

c) List the characters in each paragraph.

7

Summarize the story. The notes taken above can help you. → **S1** Checklist Summary

8

a) Describe Fatima's attitude and behaviour towards the different characters in the story and vice versa. Take notes:

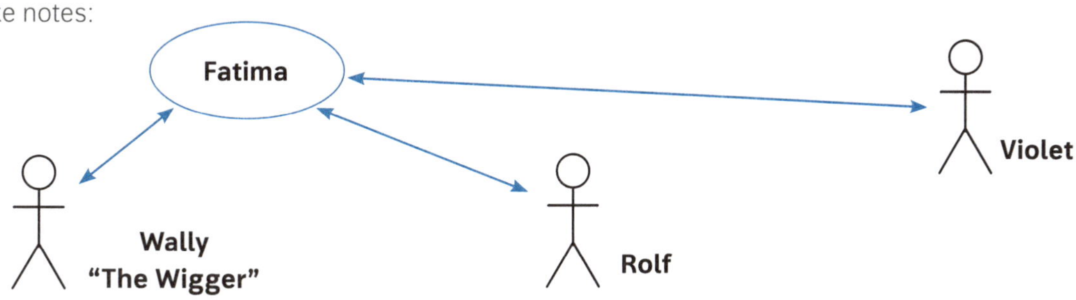

____

____

____

____

____

____

b) Characterize Fatima. Use the notes from above and write a coherent text. Pay attention to both indirect and direct characterization. Look again at the box from exercise 3 in the "Cicada" section on p. 65.

> Tip You can find types of characterization in *Camden Town Oberstufe* on p. 244 and language support for writing about characters on p. 353.

9 CHOOSE

Imagine you are Fatima. You want to explain the whole situation to Violet after the encounter at the cinema. As your attempts to call Violet have failed, you try to contact her in one of the two ways:

a) You surprise Violet by standing at her front door. Write a dialogue.

OR

b) You write her a letter. → **S2** Checklist: Creative writing

MEDIATION

10

Your American friend Bob has read "Fatima, the Biloquist: A transformation story" and is thinking about one of the themes of the short story. Fatima blames Wally "The Wigger" for *cultural appropriation*[1] and, in a way, Violet blames Fatima for adapting "the white" culture.
He wants to know whether *cultural appropriation* is also discussed in Germany. You have found an article in which there is an interview between the white journalist Robin and the black journalist Malcolm. Sum up Malcolm's opinion as to why cultural appropriation should be taken seriously and not used thoughtlessly. Write Bob an Email listing Malcolm's dos and don'ts.

→ **S19** How to improve your mediation skills

Annotations

[1] **cultural appropriation** = It is the inappropriate or unacknowledged adoption of an element of a culture or identity by members of another group. Members of a dominant group here would exploit a feature of a minority culture.

Warum Cultural Appropriation uns alle angeht

Warum verletzt es ***People of Color****, wenn weiße Menschen sich dunkel schminken oder Dreadlocks tragen? Unser weißer Autor Robin befragt seinen schwarzen Kollegen Malcolm, wieso wir [****Cultural Appropriation****] ernst nehmen sollten.*

„Die besagte Debatte ist ja mal komplett unnötig", „Sowas Lächerliches habe ich selten gehört" und „Irgendwann ist auch mal gut". Diese Kommentare finden sich häufig, wenn kulturelle Aneignung von Künstler*innen wie bei Apache 207[2] oder Shirin David[3] thematisiert werden. *Cultural Appropriation* heißt, dass sich Menschen der dominanten Gesellschaftsgruppen aus Mode, Slang-Wörtern oder sonstigen kulturellen Elementen einer Minderheitskultur bedienen, weil sie es einfach cool finden oder damit sogar Geld zu verdienen.

Aber wann ist eine Inspiration ein respektvolles Zitat und wann unangebrachte Aneignung? [...] Wir lassen unseren weißen Autoren Robin mit seinem schwarzen Kollegen Malcolm über Privilegien und Ignoranz sprechen.

Robin: Viele Kunstschaffende zitieren andere Künstler*innen. Warum sehen das *People of Color* bei der weißen Rapperin Shirin David besonders kritisch und sprechen von kultureller Aneignung?

Malcolm: [...] Shirin David bekommt zusätzliche Aufmerksamkeit dafür, dass sie sich die Haut dunkler gefärbt hat für ein Musikvideo und Haarflecht-Frisuren trägt. [...] Ihre gesamte Ästhetik, ihr Style, ihre Arbeit basiert auf den Blaupausen von schwarzen Frauen. Sie zeigt sich aber anderweitig nicht solidarisch und setzt sich in keiner Form für die Menschen ein, von denen sie finanziell profitiert. Es entsteht der Eindruck, sie schmückt sich einfach damit. [...]

Robin: Warum verletzt es manche Schwarze und *People of Color*, wenn Weiße sich dunkel schminken oder eine Haarflecht-Frisur tragen?

Malcolm: Für Menschen, wie mich zum Beispiel, ist dunkle Hautfarbe und wie man deswegen in der Welt wahrgenommen wird, eine tagtägliche Realität und kein Schmuck, den man tragen und dann wieder ablegen kann. Wenn du als weiße Person Flechtfrisuren trägst, dich dunkler schminkst, irgendwelche Slang-Wörter benutzt oder dir die Lippen aufspritzt – das sind alles Sachen, mit denen schwarze Menschen teilweise ganz schlimme, traumatische Erfahrungen gemacht haben.

Ich hatte zum Beispiel mal Dreadlocks und wurde meine ganze Schulzeit dafür gehänselt. Ich wurde mit Affen verglichen und hieß ganz lange einfach „Palmenkopf". [...]

Robin: Gibt es keine Möglichkeiten, wie ich als weiße Person schwarze Kultur feiern kann, ohne gleich kulturelle Aneignung zu betreiben?

Malcolm: [...] Ein interessantes Beispiel ist zum Beispiel Gentleman. Eine weiße Person, die aus Deutschland ist und jamaikanische Musik macht. Er hat nie Dreadlocks getragen, hat sich nie braun angemalt. Für ihn ist das keine Phase, das ist sein Leben und trotzdem ist für jeden ersichtlich, dass er weiß ist und ein Bewunderer. Der macht das nicht nur für ein Album. Gentleman zeigt Respekt und bietet vielen jamaikanischen Künstler*innen eine Bühne. Er setzt sich für schwarze Menschen und gegen Rassismus ein. Die Leute haben ihn als Teil der Szene akzeptiert. [...] Und nochmal zu Shirin David: Wenn sie das alles so geil findet, hätte sie zum Beispiel auch schwarze Rapperinnen in ihrem Album featuren oder sich mit Rassismus beschäftigen können. Dazu gehört dann auch zu markieren, dass man eben nicht schwarz ist. [...]

Robin: Warum findest du es wichtig, die Hautfarbe bei kultureller Aneignung zu thematisieren?

Malcolm: Es ist wichtig, dass weißen Menschen, wie dir, der Spiegel vorgehalten wird, damit sie lernen, dass sie weiß sind. *People of Color* wissen ihr ganzes Leben lang, dass sie schwarz bzw. nicht weiß sind. Aber wenn man immer der Standard ist, weiß man nicht, welche Vorteile und auch Ignoranz das mit sich bringt. Weiße müssen lernen, sich ihrer Hautfarbe bewusst zu werden, wenn sie empathischer sein wollen.

Robin: Was empfiehlst du mir als weißer Person?

Malcolm: Sehr wichtig ist Zuhören. Wenn du selber nicht dieser gesellschaftlichen Gruppe angehörst, die du kulturell spannend findest, dann höre diesen Leuten zu. Wenn du keinen Menschen in deinem Umfeld findest, dann gibt es auf Youtube und Instagram ganz viel Content. Check mal deine Social Media-Profile und analysiere, wem du folgst. [...] Außerdem gibt es wirklich sehr viele Bücher von Betroffenen, die du lesen kannst.

Annotations

[2] **Apache 207** = German rapper

[3] **Shirin David** = German rapper and YouTuber

Info

Identity

Self-fashioning describes a term coined by literary historian Stephen Greenblatt in 1980. It actually describes how in the Renaissance era noblemen constructed their own identity and public appearance according to a set of socially acceptable standards. Then, in public they would present themselves with good manners, wear fashionable clothes and demonstrate that they were well educated.
Self-fashioning can be adapted to the modern world. A way to present yourself differently in society. Your own identity is shaped by a great many factors such as your family, friends, classmates, peers, your education, the music you listen to, the clothes you wear, the sports you play, the media you consume and much more.

11

a) What do Violet and Fatima's self-fashioning look like? Explain Violet's self-fashioning and Fatima's self-fashioning before and after she meets Violet. Describe their "identities" by taking notes. Use quotations from the text. → **S23** How to quote

	Fatima	Violet
music		
clothes, sport		
media, others		

b) Now, describe your "identity".
Would you say you present yourself differently in different social contexts?
If so, in which and how far?

myself

12 CHALLENGE

The Fresh Prince of Bel-Air

The 90s TV-show "The Fresh Prince of Bel-Air" is mentioned in the story. After Violet has taken Fatima under her wing, Fatima watches the show on rotation and claims that she "[felt] assured that if Ashley Banks could, after five seasons, become almost as cool as Will, then she could, too." (ll. 194-195)

a) Do a research on the show, look at a synopsis and if you can watch an episode or two. You can find links to a synopsis here: **Webcode DSW-73685-10**

b) To what extent is the TV show relevant for the short story at hand? Pay attention to the theme, characters and the question of identity.

13 CHOOSE

Group work Discuss one of the following statements:

Fatima takes advantage of her friend Violet.

OR

Violet forces Fatima into something she did not want in the first place.

OR

Throughout the story Fatima struggles with her identity.

14

a) Comment on what the black girl Kayla's reaction in an online reading group tells you about the relevance of the short story and its potential message.

b) **Pair work** What other messages could the story have?

> "Growing up, I was always told from my own people that I acted like a 'white girl'. This always made me upset, but I have since learned that there is no set way to be a black girl."

LOOKING AT BOTH SHORT STORIES

15

Pair work Compare the two stories "Cicada" and "Fatima". What similarities are there and what differences can you identify? → **Language support** Comparing, p. 16

16

Look again at the info box on the topic page 57 and explain what behaviour Ellery, Fatima and Violet are confronted with.

17

Group work To what extent do the two short stories deal with the topic of black female identity?

The Founder

PRE-VIEWING

1

You are going to watch the film *The Founder*, which was directed by John Lee Hancock (2016).

a) Look at the film poster and the film still below.

b) What do you think? What will the film be about? What kind of person may the protagonist Ray Kroc be? Make a mind map and note down your first ideas about the film.

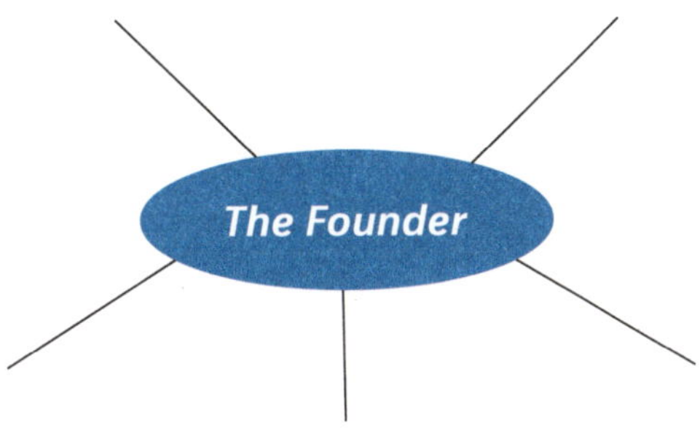

WHILE VIEWING

2

Look at the plot diagram and read the information below.
While you are watching the film, take notes and complete the plot diagram with the most important information.

Info

A **plot diagram** – key terms explained:

Exposition: the introduction of the setting, the situation and the main characters
Rising action: an important moment for the protagonist; the events focus on a conflict or a problem
Conflict: a dramatic struggle between two forces; for example, character vs. character, character vs. society, or an inner conflict
Climax: the point of highest tension; the turning point, which can change the protagonist's fate
Falling action: the tension decreases and the main problem starts to resolve, leading to the ultimate resolution
Resolution: the point when the conflict is finally (re)solved or determined unsolvable

The Founder **– Plot diagram:**

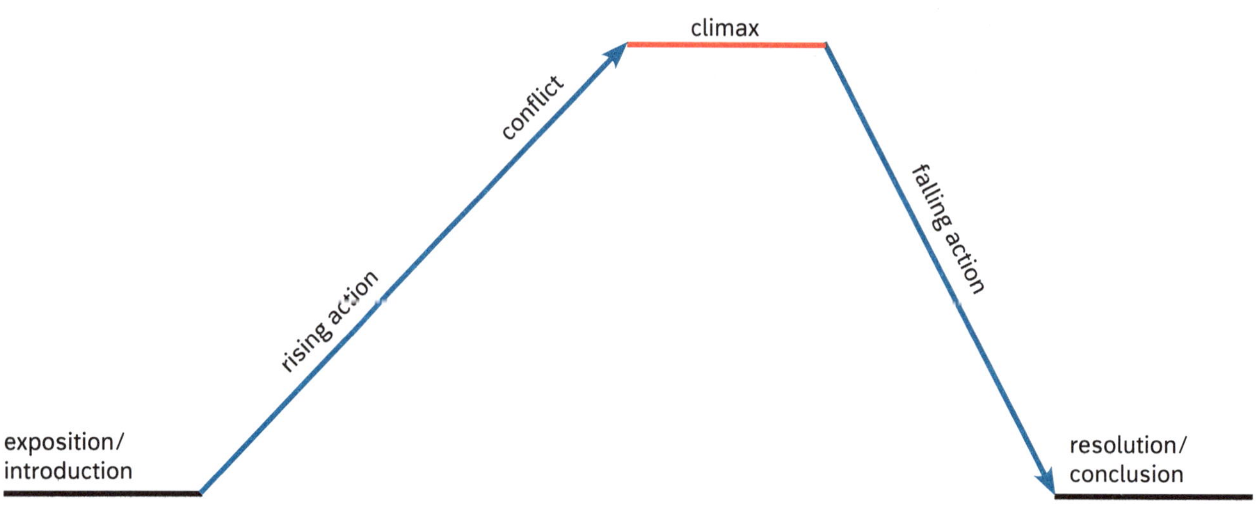

3

a) Sum up what the McDonald brothers tell Ray Kroc about their concept and the history of their business. (You can watch the following scenes again: 0:13:00 – 0:24:08)
b) Write a blog post on the McDonald brothers' idea. You can include your own experiences as a customer going to a restaurant.
→ **S7** Checklist: Writing a blog post

4
Explain how Ray Kroc manages to make Dick and Mac McDonald's concept so successful.
You can create a chart to illustrate your findings.

5 Pair work
From the very first day, a pillar of McDonald's success has been quality management (QM). In the film Ray Kroc is shocked when he realizes that some of his franchisees and people who work in his restaurants do not stick to his quality standards.
What forms of quality management do you think are most important for McDonald's? Explain why.
The key words on the right can help you.

safety | supplies | food | products | cleanliness | financial | ...

6
a) Examine what skills and qualities Ray thinks people who want to work for McDonald's should have.

responsible | curious | fair | conscientious | stress-resistant | well-organized | highly motivated | reliable | resilient | sociable | cooperative | diligent | modest | independent | flexible | calm | determined | practical | creative | open-minded | ...

b) Write a job ad that Ray could have written. → **S8** How to improve your text

7 → **S16** Checklist: Analysis of a film scene → **Workshop** Analysing a feature film
Watch the scene "Welcome to Minneapolis" (0:57:08 – 0:58:07) again.

Ray Kroc and Fred Turner have just landed in Minneapolis and a taxi has taken them to the opening of a new McDonald's franchise. The music starts, there is a close-up of Ray's shoe stepping out of the car, a tilting shot follows and the camera moves upwards – and Ray gets out of the car.

a) Describe your first impression of the scene.

b) Describe the two film stills and the cinematic effects used.

c) Analyse how Ray is presented in the scene and how the film-makers have accomplished this.

8 → **S16** Checklist: Analysis of a film scene → **Workshop** Analysing a feature film

a) Watch the scene in which Ray buys Dick and Mac out. Complete the viewing log below (you don't need to fill in every single box). You can look up cinematic devices on pp. 87–88 in your book.

time	setting/characters	what is going on/ what they are talking about	cinematic devices	function/effect
1:34:25 – 1:34:28	a dark conference room; Dick and Mac and their lawyer, Ray and his lawyer	the business partners and their lawyers are sitting at a table; Ray's lawyer explains that he agrees to the brothers' conditions of sale but with one exception	tracking shot from right to left, starting from behind the stairs; full shot of the conference table; the lighting is quite dark, shady	voyeuristic, it seems as if the viewer witnesses the scene from some distance
1:34:29 – 1:34:33		the 1% royalty for the brothers won't be written into the contract		
1:34:34 – 1:34:36		Mac is shocked and turns his head to his brother and back to Ray		
1:34:37 – 1:34:41			close-up of Ray	
1:34:41 – 1:34:44			close-up of Mac	
1:34:45 – 1:34:48			close-up of Ray	
1:34:49 – 1:34:57		Ray promises that the brothers will get their full royalties	quick shots showing close-ups of Dick, Mac and Ray	

time	setting/characters	what is going on/ what they are talking about	cinematic devices	function/effect
1:34:58 – 1:34:59			over the shoulder shot showing Dick, Mac and their lawyer	
1:35:00 – 1:35:02		Ray stands up and gives them his word	full shot of the conference table from below the stairs	
1:35:03 – 1:35:21			quick shots showing close-ups of Ray, Mac, including Ray's outstretched hand, and Dick; medium shot: Ray standing, the others sitting at the table	
1:35:22 – 1:35:25	Ray and his lawyer			
1:35:26 – 1:35:34			close-up of Mac	
1:35:34 – 1:35:49	Dick and Mac		medium shot, filmed through a glass pane; close-up of the cheques	

b) Analyse the scene focusing on the characters' emotions, the audience's possible reaction and how those are created through acting and cinematic devices.

9 → **S1** Checklist: Summary

Write a plot summary of the film *The Founder*. You can use your plot diagram from p. 86.

POST-VIEWING

10 **Pair work**

a) At the beginning of the film, Ray is listening to the motivational record "The Power of the Positive" by Dr. Clarence Floyd Nelson (0:04:15 – 0:06:25). Read the extract from the film script below. Assess to what extent the scene foreshadows Ray's character traits and the way he acts to reach his goals.

> "Persistence. Nothing in the world can take the place of persistence.
> Talent won't. Nothing is more common than unsuccessful men with talent.
> Genius won't. Unrewarded genius is practically a cliché.
> Education won't. The world is full of educated fools.
> Persistence and determination alone are all powerful.
> Show that you don't have to be defeated by anything. That you can have peace of mind, improved health and a never ceasing flow of energy. If you attempt each and every day to achieve these things, the results will make themselves obvious to you. While it may sound like a magical notion, it is in you to create your own future. The greatest discovery of my generation is that human beings can alter their lives by altering their attitudes of mind.
> Or as Ralph Waldo Emerson declared, "A man is what he thinks about all day long.""

b) Compare this scene with the end of the film, when Ray is practising his speech in front of the mirror (1:39:25 – 1:40:20).

c) Comment on whether you agree or disagree with this attitude that persistence and determination are more important than talent or education in the world of work.

11 → **Workshop** Analysing characters → **S8** How to improve your text

Write a coherent text to characterize Ray.

12

Analyse the development of Ray's relationship with his wife Ethel.

13 → **Workshop** Analysing characters → **S8** How to improve your text

Choose one of the following characters and write a characterization.

- Fred Turner
- Harry Sonneborn
- Ethel Kroc
- Joan Kroc (previously Smith)
- Dick McDonald
- Mac McDonald

14

a) **Pair work** Choose two of the following quotes by Ray Kroc and explain in what contexts in the film they are said.

> "McDonald's can be the new American church. Feeding bodies and feeding souls and it ain't just open on Sundays, boys. It's open seven days a week." (0:34:04 – 0:34:18)

> "Contracts are like hearts, they're made to be broken." (1:25:53 – 1:25:57)

> "Business is war. It's dog eat dog, rat eat rat. If my competitor were drowning, I'd walk over and I'd put a hose right in his mouth." (1:29:24 – 1:29:33)

> "Now, I know what you're thinking. How the heck does a 52-year-old, over the hill, milkshake machine salesman, build a fast food empire with 1600 restaurants, in 50 states, five foreign countries, with an annual revenue of in the neighborhood of 700 million dollars? One word, persistence." (1:39:25 – 1:39:52)

b) **Group work** Comment on the quotes: which ones do you agree or disagree with? Give reasons for your answers.

15 **Group work**

Discuss whether Ray Kroc can be considered an exceptional founder.
Comment on the film title, too.

16

Film directors and screenwriters often adapt real facts for a more dramatic effect, which is called 'artistic licence'. What is fiction and what is reality? What may be exaggerated, what was left out, what did not really happen? Check some facts and research how accurate the film is if you compare it with the historic events.

Ray Kroc, Chairman of the Board of the McDonald's Corporation

Fiction?	Reality?

17

a) Write a film review on *The Founder*.

Info

Tips on how to write a film review:

- Come up with a catchy heading for your review.
- Name essential information about the film (title, release date, genre, director, screenwriter, producer).
- Give a short plot summary, but do not give away too much of the story (such as a twist or the end) as you might spoil the film for a possible audience.
- Describe your personal impression of the film.
- Comment on the actors. (Were they convincing? Were they a good choice for the roles?)
- Describe how the cinematic devices contribute to the effect of the film (e.g. camera, editing, lighting, sound, special effects, ...).
- Finally, say whether you would recommend the film (and, if so, to whom/what kind of audience). Give the film a rating (1–10 stars) and explain your decision.

b) Use the internet to find out how other viewers have rated the film. Think about whether you would like to upload your film review, too.

The American Dream

1
Read the information below.

Info

The American Dream

The American Dream is a concept that generations of people in the United States have believed in and strived for. The term was coined by James Truslow Adams in his book *The Epic of America* (1931):
"The American Dream is that dream of a land in which life should be better and richer and fuller for everyone, with opportunity for each according to ability or achievement."
The American Dream is rooted in the Declaration of Independence (July 4, 1776), a document signed by the Thirteen Colonies seeking independence from British rule:
"We hold these truths to be self-evident, that all men are created equal, that they are endowed by their Creator with certain unalienable Rights, that among these are Life, Liberty and the pursuit of Happiness."
– Preamble to the Declaration of Independence
For many people, the American Dream means that everybody has the freedom to do what they want and everybody who works hard can be successful and rise "from rags to riches".

2 Group work
There is a variety of individual interpretations of the American Dream, for example:

- getting rich, making it
- climbing up the social ladder
- leading a happy life
- living peacefully
- having a happy family and home
- being independent
- knowing that everything is possible
- doing what you love
- being able to do good in the world
- being self-employed
- owning your own company
- practising your religion freely
- being able to say your opinion
- being treated equally, no matter who you are or where you are from
- ...

What do you think about the American Dream and the different interpretations? Can the American Dream come true for everybody? Discuss in your group.

3 Pair work
What is the American Dream for the following characters from the film *The Founder*? What is similar and what is different? Note down some ideas and fill in the Venn diagram below.

The American Dream for characters in *The Founder*

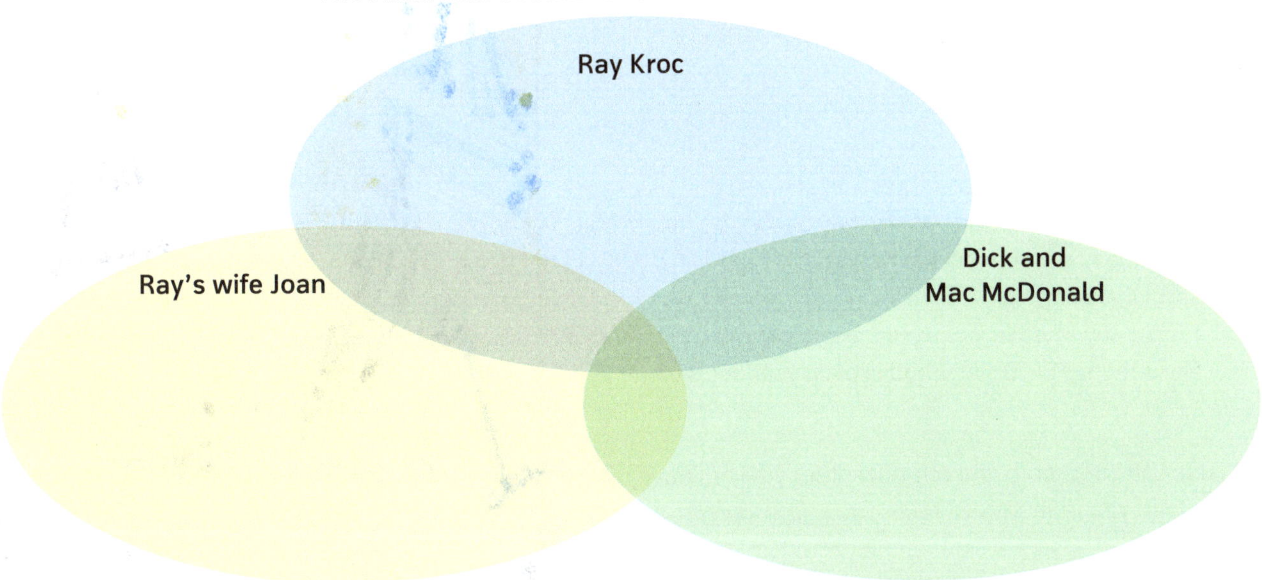

4 Pair work

You are going to watch the CNBC video "Why McDonald's Failed In Iceland".

a) Pre-viewing: As the title of the documentary suggests, McDonald's tried to establish their business in Iceland. Despite being successful in more than 100 countries around the world, they failed in Iceland. Name possible reasons. Share your ideas with a partner.

b) Now watch the video. **Webcode** DSW-73685-11
While you are watching, list the reasons for McDonald's failure in Iceland. Compare your assumptions from a) with the actual reasons. Which aspects were you right about and which aspects were you wrong about?

c) Post-viewing: Imagine McDonald's wants to return to Iceland and make another attempt to establish their franchise there. Fill in the grid below. Then write a short text giving some advice to the McDonald's management.

McDonald's in Iceland?	
Things they can count on	**Hurdles to overcome**
- high demand - Finding employees - customers	- economic situation in Iceland - high costs (import) - new attempt → that it will be accepted

Ethics in the world of business

1

Research online how McDonald's presents itself as a company. Find out more about their beliefs and values, priorities and activities. Present your findings in class.

2 → **Workshop** Analysing a cartoon → **S17** How to work with cartoons

Look at the cartoon and describe it. Explain the message of the cartoon.

"Hangin' around McDonald's again, aren't you?"

3 → **S15** How to describe pictures

McDonald's has been criticised for different reasons. Look at the photos below and describe the different forms of protest against McDonald's.

4

Use the internet to find out more about the different reasons why McDonald's has been criticised. Present your findings in class.

5 Pair work

Examine how both positive and negative aspects of McDonald's are presented in the film *The Founder*.

6 Group work

Discuss whether or not you would like to work for McDonald's. Give reasons for your answers.

7 → **S3** Checklist: Formal letter

Choose an international company that you find interesting. Use the internet to find out more about the company, their beliefs and values, and possible careers. Write a letter of application to the company.

MEDIATION

8 → **Workshop** Mediation → **S19** How to improve your mediation skills → **S5** Checklist: Writing a speech

You are taking part in an international youth conference on environmental protection and sustainability. Read the article from the online magazine *BASIC thinking*. Use the information to prepare a speech for the conference. Explain how McDonald's has been working on changing its image in Germany and how the company can still improve.

Wie nachhaltig ist McDonald's Deutschland wirklich?

30. Mrz 2021
geschrieben von Marinela Potor

Im Klimacheck von *BASIC thinking* stellen wir die Nachhaltigkeitsstrategien von Konzernen auf den Prüfstand. Wie nachhaltig und grün sind die neuen Konzepte wirklich? Diesmal: McDonald's Deutschland.

Es war ein großes Zeichen, als McDonald's im Februar 2021 eine dreijährige Partnerschaft mit Beyond Meat ankündigte. Das Unternehmen für vegane Produkte soll für McDonald's weltweit den pflanzlichen McPlant-Burger liefern.
Solche Kooperationen sind fürs Klima weitreichender als man denkt. Sie signalisieren schließlich Produzenten und Lieferanten weltweit, dass der Trend weg vom Fleisch und hin zu pflanzenbasierter Ernährung geht.
Und auch McDonald's positioniert sich damit als Unternehmen, das verstärkt auf Klimaschutz achten will. Doch wie sieht das über den veganen Burger hinaus aus? Wir schauen uns die aktuelle Nachhaltigkeitsstrategie der Fast-Food-Kette in Deutschland an. [...]

Regionale Priorität
Tatsächlich hat sich McDonald's Deutschland hier sehr bewusst für eine möglichst regionale Versorgung entschieden. Bis auf Tomaten, Zwiebeln, Kaffee sowie Shrimps und Fisch, die aus Europa oder aus weltweiten Quellen stammen, kommt die Mehrheit der Produkte aus Deutschland.
Das reduziert natürlich Lieferwege. Als Qualitätssiegel setzt McDonald's auf Nachhaltigkeitszertifikate.

Bio-Siegel und Co.
Dazu gehört das Bio-Siegel bei Obst und Gemüse. Das ist natürlich nicht das strikteste aller Nachhaltigkeitssiegel, aber immerhin.
Fischprodukte stammen zu 100 Prozent per MSC-Label und ASC-Label aus nachhaltiger Fischerei und der Kaffee kommt von Farmen, die zur Rainforest-Alliance gehören.

Tierhaltung
Bei den Hühnern achtet das Unternehmen darauf, dass die Tiere mit gentechnisch unveränderten vegetarischen Futtermitteln gefüttert werden und der Einsatz von Antibiotika gemindert wird. Heißt aber auch: Die Hähnchenprodukte sind nicht durchweg frei von Antibiotika.
Zur Tierhaltung der Hühner sagte McDonald's gegenüber *BASIC thinking*, dass alle Hühnerprodukte zu 100 Prozent von Tieren aus Freilandhaltung kämen.
Für Rindfleisch gibt es seit 2019 das Programm „Best Beef". Damit fördert das Unternehmen Rindbauern, die in ihren Nachhaltigkeitsansätzen über das gesetzlich erforderliche Minimum hinausgehen.
Das Schweinefleisch kommt sowohl von männlichen (nicht-kastrierten) und weiblichen Tieren und stammt aus dem Qualitätsprogramm QS. Dazu gehören sowohl artgerechte Fütterung als auch Transport.
Wie bereits erwähnt ist auch die neue Partnerschaft mit Beyond Meat und dem Ausrollen von veganen Burgern ein weiterer Aspekt für mehr Klimaschutz. Ebenfalls positiv: Den Januar 2021 erklärte McDonald's zum „Veganuary."

Verpackung
Als Fast-Food-Kette sind Verpackungen für McDonald's natürlich ein großes Thema. Hier hat das Unternehmen aber bereits einen grünen Ansatz.
Dessertverpackungen (Strohhalme, Eisbecher, Löffel) sind schon komplett plastikfrei. Für Einwegbecher (aus Papier) gibt es ein Recyclingprogramm, um daraus bedruckbare Papierbögen zu machen.
Die Happy-Meal-Verpackungen sind noch nicht komplett plastikfrei. Doch man bemüht sich, zunehmend mehr Papier und weniger Plastik zu nutzen.
Das Spielzeug ist aber weiterhin aus Plastik. [...]

Einweg-Papier ist auch Verschwendung
Klar ist: Diese Strategie stammt vor der neuen Vorgabe der Bundesregierung, die Einweg-Plastik verbietet. Tatsächlich hat McDonald's sein Plastikproblem aber schon so gut wie gelöst. Nur: Auch

Einweg-Papier ist im Grunde Ressourcenvergeudung. Bis 2025 soll es aber nur noch Verpackungen aus erneuerbarem, recyceltem oder zertifiziertem Material geben. [...]

Energie

Im Bereich „Energie" konzentriert sich die Nachhaltigkeitsstrategie des Konzerns in Deutschland vor allem auf zwei Säulen: Mobilität und Strom.

Ökostrom und E-Autos

So nutzen die Betriebe in Deutschland zu 100 Prozent Strom aus Wasserkraft. [...] Beim eigenen Fuhrpark setzt sich der Konzern Grenzwerte und bemüht sich zumindest die E-Flotte auszubauen. [...]

So bietet das Unternehmen seinen Mitarbeitern auch ein günstiges Fahrradleasing an (auch mit E-Bikes). Auch bei den Lieferungen setzt McDonald's in Deutschland offenbar auf zwei Räder. [...]

Fazit zur Nachhaltigkeitsstrategie von McDonald's in Deutschland

Verglichen mit den Anfängen von McDonald's hat die Fast-Food-Kette einen großen Wandel vollzogen. Klar: Schnelles Essen ist immer noch das Konzept und allein das mögen viele aus Klimasicht kritisieren.

Dennoch bemüht sich die Restaurantkette eindeutig um einen niedrigeren CO_2-Fußabdruck. In vielen Bereichen, wie etwa beim Recycling, Ökostrom oder der regionalen Produkt- und Lieferkette ist schon ein großes Bewusstsein für den Klimaschutz zu erkennen, auch wenn sicherlich noch Luft nach oben besteht.

Lobenswert ist auch der Transparenz-Ansatz des Unternehmens. Wer will, findet online oder per App eine detaillierte Auflistung aller Zutaten in den einzelnen Produkten. [...]

Wasserstrategie fehlt

Auffällig ist aber, dass McDonald's bestimmte Bereiche in seiner Nachhaltigkeitsstrategie gar nicht erst erwähnt.

Dazu gehören zum Beispiel:

- die Zubereitung der Gerichte
- Zusatzstoffe in Gerichten
- Wasserkonsum

Wie viel Wasser verbraucht McDonald's Deutschland beispielsweise in der gesamten Produktkette? Gibt es Ansätze, um Wasser zu sparen oder auch wenn möglich zu recyceln?

Auf Nachfrage von *BASIC thinking* sagt das Unternehmen, dass verantwortungsbewusstes Wassermanagement durchaus Teil der Nachhaltigkeitsstrategie sei.

„In Deutschland folgen wir diesem Grundsatz. So wurden unsere Restaurants unter anderem mit entsprechenden Reinigungsanlagen ausgestattet, um eine Abwasserbelastung möglichst zu minimieren", sagt das Unternehmen gegenüber *BASIC thinking*.

Was ist mit Plastikflaschen?

Und: Was ist eigentlich mit den Wasser- und Getränkeprodukten in den Restaurants? Diese werden nach wie vor in Plastik verpackt. Auch hier könnte sich die Kette künftig nachhaltigere Alternativen überlegen, die es ja durchaus gibt.

Dazu sagt McDonald's Deutschland Folgendes: „Apfelschorle und Wasser werden derzeit in Einwegpfandgebinden angeboten, da diese aus Verpackungs- und Recyclingprozessgesichtspunkten so bestmöglich in einen optimierten und geschlossenen Kreislauf zurückgeführt werden können."

Angesichts eines sehr guten Mehrwegsystems von Glasflaschen in Deutschland, ist dies aber nicht zu 100 Prozent nachvollziehbar.

Soziale Verantwortung von Fast Food

Die Zutaten der Gerichte wie Transfette, Zucker oder auch Stärken mögen etwa im Vergleich zu Fleisch keinen extremen Klimaeffekt haben. Doch sie schaden den Konsumentinnen und Konsumenten.

Menschen, die sehr viel Fast Food konsumieren, leiden öfter an Depressionen, ihre Haut altert schneller und Fast Food begünstigt auch Krankheiten wie Diabetes Typ 2 und Demenz.

Fairerweise muss man dazu sagen, dass dies meist daran liegt, dass Menschen, die viel Fast Food essen auch wenig Sport treiben und anderweitig ungesund unterwegs sind. Auch wird mal ein Burger hier oder dort keine Langzeitschäden hervorrufen.

Dennoch gäbe es in diesen Bereichen durchaus noch Verbesserungspotenzial für McDonald's. Darin steckt aber auch eine wirtschaftliche Herausforderung. Denn als günstige Fast-Food-Kette hat McDonald's natürlich auch einen strikten Price-Point.

Wer will schon so viel für einen Burger bei „Mickie D's" zahlen wie in einem Gourmet-Restaurant?

McDonald's muss mit der Zeit gehen

Gleichzeitig sieht natürlich auch der Konzern, dass sich das Bewusstsein der Kundinnen und Kunden wandelt, hin zu mehr Nachhaltigkeit und einem gesünderen Lifestyle. Fettige Pommes sind da einfach nicht mehr zeitgemäß.

Es wird daher spannend zu sehen, wie McDonald's künftig mit den Verbraucherinnen und Verbrauchern mitgehen wird und gleichzeitig wirtschaftlich bleiben kann.

Notes for your speech:

PRE-VIEWING

London versus Wales – city versus country life

The settings of the film *Pride* are urban London on the one hand and a remote village called Onllwyn in Wales on the other hand.

	London, UK	Onllwyn in Wales, UK
area	1572 km^2	10,83 km^2
population	9.002.488	1.214
density of population	5,701 / km^2	112,1 / km^2
official language(s)	English	English & Welsh

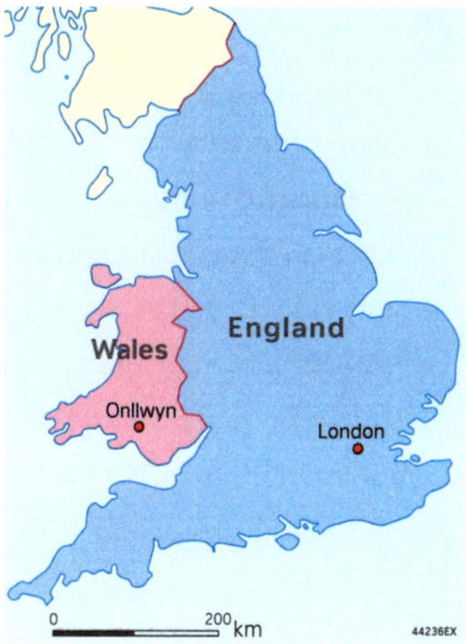

1

a) On your own, imagine how life might be in a city like London in comparison to life in a village like Onllwyn in Wales. Consider ...
- amusement and leisure activities,
- population,
- cultural diversity,
- community feeling,
- facilities and shops,
- the opportunity of employment,
- landscape / environment,
- ...

b) In class, place yourselves on a position line: living in an urban city like London versus living in a remote village like Onllwyn. Discuss where you would rather like to live. Give reasons.

Language support

Discussing

voicing an opinion	highlighting facts	giving examples and linking arguments
• Well, if you ask me ... • As far as I'm concerned ... / My (personal) view is that ... • Personally, I think / believe / suppose ... • I am of mixed opinions (about / on) ...	• The fact is that ... • The (main) point is that ... • There is no doubt that ...	• There are various / several reasons for ... • For instance ... / For example ... • On the one hand, ... On the other hand, ... • First, ... / Second, ... • That is why ... / Because of ...
agreeing	**partially agreeing**	**disagreeing**
• I simply must agree with that. • I completely / absolutely agree with ... • How very true. / Yes, indeed.	• That seems obvious, but ... • Under certain circumstances ... • I can understand ... but ... • I see what you mean, but it seems to me ... • I am able to relate to what you're saying. However, I would suggest ...	• I (very much) doubt whether ... • I am of a different opinion because ... • I cannot share this view. • Unlike ... I think ...

Cartoon analysis – gay life in cities and remote areas

2

a) Analyse the characters and objects in the cartoon and explain its message.
→ **S17** How to work with cartoons

Language support

Talking about a cartoon

- The cartoon illustrates / shows / depicts / deals with / refers to / comments on / points out ...
- In the cartoon there is / are ... / seems to be ... ... | One can see ...
- At the top / at the back / at the front / at the bottom ... | In the middle / in the centre ... | On the right / on the left / in the top left-hand corner / in the bottom right-hand corner ...
- It can be assumed that ... because it brings its message across by ...
- The cartoonist tries to / intends to / is making fun of / criticizes / draws attention to ...

b) Speculate and comment on the acceptance of gay-life in cities like London versus gay-life in remote areas like Onllwyn.

The decline of the coal mining industry

3

Not only gay people, but also miners had to fight against discrimination and were denied social and political acceptance. The coal mining industry used to be a big player in British economy. However, things have changed.
Take a look at the bar chart and describe the overall development of employees in the coal mining industry in the UK. → **S18** How to analyse statistics

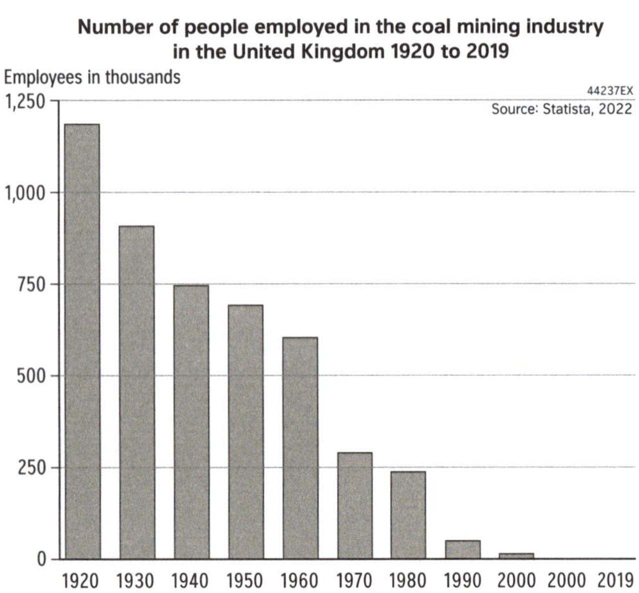

Language support

Analyzing tables, graphs and charts

- The bar chart is about ... / shows the distribution of ... / presents ... / provides information on / deals with ..., covering a period of ...
- It is taken from ... / The source of the data is ... | ... was published by ... on ...
- The figures show / reveal how ... is divided / made up.
- All the figures are given as percentages / total numbers.
- The highest / lowest figure / score ... | The figures reach a peak ... / show a steep / strong / rapid growth / decline ... / grow / decline by ... %.
- The chart shows an increase / a growth (of) | a decline (in) ... / a decrease (in) ...
- Almost no ... / Only a few ... / Less than ...
- All in all / By and large, the statistics for ... reveal / show / present / indicate ...
- This development clearly indicates that ...

4

a) Read the lyric excerpt from the song "Solidarity forever" and identify its main message.

b) Discuss in how far the song can be connected to the employment situation of the coal miners (see the bar chart on p. 100)?

c) **Pair work** Speculate (1) about the reasons for the decline in employment and (2) the changes and problems that might have followed – especially in the 1980s and 1990s.

Chorus:
Solidarity forever
Solidarity forever
Solidarity forever
For the union[1] makes us strong
[...]

It is we who plowed[2] the prairies, built the cities where they trade;
Dug the mines and built the workshops, endless miles of railroad laid;
Now we stand outcast[3] and starving midst the wonders we have made;
But the union makes us strong.

Chorus:
[...]
They have taken untold millions that they never toiled[4] to earn,
But without our brain and muscle not a single wheel can turn.
We can break their haughty[5] power, gain our freedom when we learn
That the union makes us strong.

Chorus:
In our hands is placed a power greater than their hoarded gold,
Greater than the might[6] of armies, magnified a thousand-fold[7].
We can bring to birth a new world from the ashes of the old
For the union makes us strong.

Annotations
[1] **union** = a workers' organization which represents its members and aims to improve things such as their working conditions and pay
[2] to **plow** (*AE*) = when sb ploughs an area of land, they turn over the soil using a plough
[3] **outcast** = rejected, abandoned, or discarded; cast out
[4] to **toil** = when people toil, they work very hard doing unpleasant or tiring tasks.
[5] **haughty** = arrogant
[6] **might** = bodily strength
[7] **fold** = here: multiplied by 1000

d) Do some research on the miners' strike of 1984-1985 in the UK and structure the information in a (digital) poster as follows:
- When was the strike and how long did it last?
- What was the strike about?
- Who was involved?
- Which political decisions led to the miners' strike?
- What was the NUM and which role did it play?
- What happened during the strike (media coverage, police, violence etc.)?
- What effect did the strike have on the miners' families?
- How did the strike end?

Info

Conservative Margaret Thatcher, also called the "Iron Lady", had become the UK's first female prime minister in 1979. She aimed at turning the UK's ailing[1] economy around. A key element of her strategy was to privatize state-owned companies, especially those that heavily relied on subsidies[2] like coal mines and steel factories. At the same time, she wanted to weaken the power of the trade unions[3], which she considered too powerful after the strikes of the National Union of Mine workers had repeatedly brought the country to a halt in the 1970s.

Annotations

[1] **ailing** = having or suffering from an illness or injury

[2] **subsidy** = a grant by a government to a private person or company to assist an enterprise deemed advantageous to the public

[3] **trade union** = an organization of workers formed for the purpose of advancing its members' interests in respect to wages, benefits, and working conditions

For your notes:

____

____

____

____

____

____

____

The film *Pride* – first encounters

5

Now watch the trailer for *Pride*. You can find a link here: **Webcode** DSW-73685-12

a) Point out the relationship between the Lesbians & Gays and the Miners.

b) Comment on in how far you think the title of the film reflects and thus unites these groups (the miners and the lesbian and gay people).

c) Speculate on the genre of *Pride* and state it. Give reasons for your choice.

Some examples of genres			
action	**crime**	**documentary**	**drama**
• high speed • physical stunts and chases • rescues, battles, fights, escapes • often flat heroes and villains (good guy – bad guy)	• high speed with some mystery • action of a criminal mastermind versus the rise and fall of eerie criminals	• non-fictional • reporting on an issue of interest	• serious and plot-driven • round, real-life characters and stories • intense character development and interaction • intense human emotions

Some examples of genres			
comedy	**horror**	**romance**	**suspense / mystery**
• consists mostly of humorous or amusing scenes and plotlines • sometimes includes facets of parody and / or irony and sarcasm	• large amount of violence in the plot • trying to awake audience's worst fears and nightmares about the arrival of an evil force, or event • often mythical creatures, such as ghosts, vampires, and zombies	• alternating tone from happy to tragic • love between two protagonists, e.g. love at first sight, forbidden love, love triangles and love requiring great sacrifices	• a person of authority, usually a detective, trying to solve a mysterious crime • clues, investigation, and logical reasoning • constant suspense created through visual or unusual plot twists

Revisiting Cinematography

6

In order to analyse and talk about *Pride* properly you need some film specific terms and phrases. When dealing with films, camera operations and music or sound play a vital role in guiding and influencing the viewer as intended by the film maker.
Look at the table of the most common camera operations that are used in films. Match the functions on the right to the given camera operations on the left.

Tip You can find a list of cinematic devices in *Camden Town Oberstufe* p. 87-88.

I FIELD SIZE

Camera operations		Functions
A long shot	☐	1 points out sth specific about sb / sth
B full shot	☐	2 provides a complete picture of sb / sth
C medium shot	☐	3 points out a particular detail about sb / sth
D close-up shot	☐	4 presents the setting of the scene
E extreme close-up shot	☐	5 provides a closer look at sb / sth

II CAMERA MOVEMENT

Camera operations		Functions
A static shot	☐	1 horizontal / vertical movement from a static position to shift focus towards or away from sb / sth
B zoom in / out	☐	2 creates the impression of following sb / sth
C panning / tilting shot	☐	3 no movement; creates a feeling of hesitation / calmness / slowness
D tracking shot	☐	4 puts focus on something or takes focus away

III CAMERA ANGLE AND POSITION

Camera operations		Functions
A overhead shot	☐	1 creates an overall impression of the scene
B high-angle shot / bird's eye	☐	2 creates a neutral impression
C eye-level shot	☐	3 makes sb / sth seem unimportant
D low-angle shot	☐	4 represents a character's perspective
E over-the-shoulder shot	☐	5 creates the impression of being involved in a conversation
F reverse-angle shot	☐	6 usually in connection with over-the-shoulder to show the other character's reaction / side
G point-of-view shot	☐	7 sets the scene that's to come
H establishing shot	☐	8 makes sb / sth look important

IV EDITING/MONTAGE

Camera operations		Functions
A fast cut	☐	1 opens/closes an action / scene slowly
B slow cut	☐	2 creates focus on sth specific or creates calm atmosphere
C fade in/fade out	☐	3 intensifies an action / moment
D cross-cut	☐	4 depicts action vividly
E slow motion	☐	5 focuses on contrast and thus creates suspense
F fast motion	☐	6 provides a comment on the action
G voice-over	☐	7 changes chronological order and therefore connects / disconnects action / moments
H flashback / flash forward	☐	8 focus on text and its meaning, gives additional information without adding voices or stressing the meaning of voices
I floating, superimposed text	☐	9 intensifies speed, creating the impression of change

Language support

Talking about cinematography

- The establishing shot of the film shows / portrays ... / ... is shown in a medium shot / (extreme) close-up
- ... brings the viewer closer to ... / creates a distance between ...
- The focus is on a ... in detail.
- The movement of ... is followed in a ... shot.
- The shots follow each other quickly / slowly.
- The viewer sees the character in ... / There is a close-up of the character ...
- The scene is shot from X's point of view. / ... is seen from the perspective of ...
- The director uses a long shot of the setting. / ... uses high- / low- / eye-level angel shots of ...
- The camera pans from left to right / tilts up / tilts down.

Effects of cinematography

- ... describes characters indirectly / shows a character's emotions / draws attention to sth. / describes the setting / evokes a certain atmosphere ...
- ... is presented in a low-angle shot / high-angle shot, which illustrates inferiority / vulnerability / superiority / power ...
- The point of view shots make the audience experience the (emotional) perspective of ...
- The close-up is used to focus attention on .../ reveals the character's feelings / makes the situation more intimate.
- ... is shown in a close-up so the viewer can see the reaction in his / her face when ...
- The over-the-shoulder shots include the viewers in the action.
- ... uses a fade-in / fade-out to ...
- The hand-held camera underlines ... / gives the scene an unsteady quality / aims at authenticity.
- The light used in the scene is harsh / soft / bright / intense.
- The ... is used to focus on ... / draw attention to ... / This ... emphasizes / stresses / indicates ...
- ... is used to build (up) suspense / tension / to create a certain effect / to convey a feeling of / to create a mood to set the scene.
- ... affects / touches the viewers.
- ... suggests / signifies that / provides a strong contrast to / serves as an insight into ... / bridges two scenes

WHILE VIEWING

Story line and character maps – From the Gay Pride March in 1984 to the Gay Pride March in 1985

7

a) Before watching the film, make yourself familiar with the different main characters on the internet. Describe their outward appearance in keywords so that you will know who is who in the film. You can find a link to the cast here: **Webcode** DSW-73685-13

Joe / Bromley | Cliff | Dai | Gethin | Hefina | Jonathan | Mark | Maureen | Mike | Sian | Steph

b) CHOOSE

Now you are going to watch the entire film. → **S20** How to listen / watch effectively
While watching take notes on aspects mentioned in the story map. Use your notes to write a summary which concisely answers the five w-questions (who, what, where, when and why?).
→ **S1** Checklist: Summary

OR

Focus on a preassigned character from the list in a) and take notes while watching the film referring to different aspects of characterization.
→ **S12** Checklist: Analysis – prose → **S8** How to improve your text → **Infobox** p. 65

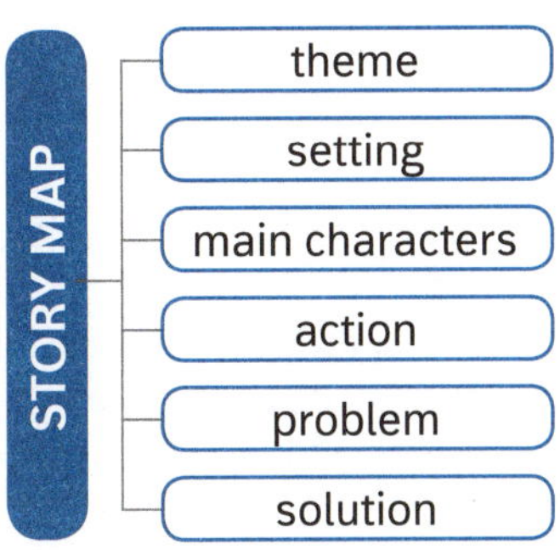

Continuously revise your findings in terms of character development and change. Be prepared to present and discuss your findings afterwards.

c) **Pair work** Compare your findings with a classmate who has been dealing with the same character. Design a suitable form of visualization (e.g., graphic organizer, mind map, poster, etc.).

d) Present your products in a Gallery Walk.

Language support

Character traits

positive traits			negative traits	
active	confident	proud	bad-tempered	malicious
affectionate	conscientious	reliable	cold-hearted	narrow-minded
ambitious	courageous	sensitive	deceitful	obnoxious
brave	dedicated	sophisticated	grouchy	old-fashioned
caring	glamorous	talkative	hypocritical	petty-minded
charismatic	honorable	tenacious	ignorant	rude
charming	humble	virtuous	impolite	self-centered
compassionate	mature	warm-hearted	jealous	stubborn
	perseverant	witty		...
		...		

8 CHALLENGE

a) **Group work** After having encountered all the individual characters in the film, design a character map of the main and minor characters in *Pride* as a graphic organizer which visualizes their interconnected relationships. Use arrows and label them with keywords or symbols.

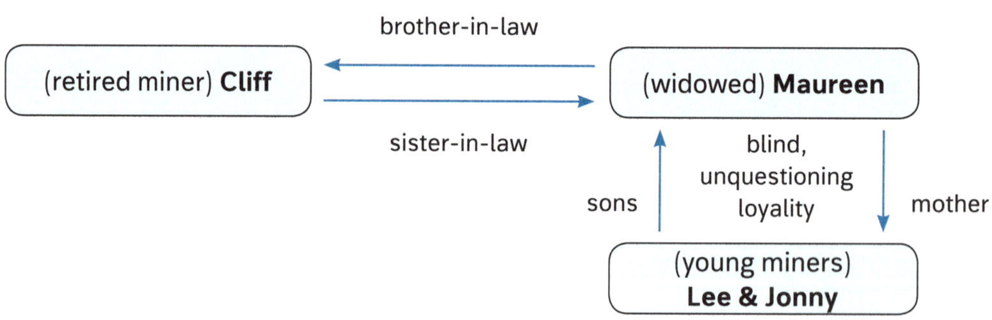

b) Write a characterisation of your assigned character.

Language support

Talking about characters

- The main / principle character in the story is ...
- Another central character is ...
- ... is characterized / described / portrayed / depicted / presented as ...
- ... proves to be ...
- As far as his character is concerned, it can be said that she / he is ...
- Concerning his / her character, it can be said that ...
- This character trait becomes apparent when ...
- The body language / The action reveals that ...
- His / Her statement "..." shows / proves / reveals that ...
- It is quite apparent that ...
- Proof of this can be found in / when ... / This is an example of ...
- He / She has many positive traits of character / characteristics.
- His / Her behaviour is marked by ....
- He / She shows ... behaviour.
- A positive / negative aspect of his / her behaviour is ...
- He / She gradually develops into ... / In the course of the film he / she undergoes a development. ... remains unchanged.
- The motive / reason / grounds for his / her action is influenced by ...
- The relationship can be described as / characterized by ...

Language support

Useful linking words			
giving examples	**adding information**	**giving reasons**	**sequencing ideas**
for example for instance such as	and as well as too in addition also furthermore moreover / apart from in addition to / besides ...	due to / due to the fact that owing to / owing to the fact that because / because of since / as	The former, ... the latter ... Firstly / Secondly / Finally ... The following ... Last but not least ...
giving a result	**contrasting ideas**	**comparing ideas**	**summarizing**
therefore so / consequently this means that as a result / the result is that is why hence thus	but / however / although / even though / despite / despite the fact that / in spite of / in spite of the fact that / nevertheless nonetheless / while / whereas	similarly equally likewise in the same way	in short / in brief to summarize / to sum up in a nutshell to conclude / in conclusion / all in all / on the whole

Stay in the closet

9 Think-Pair-Share

a) **Think** Point out which animosities towards gay people are presented and how they are depicted in *Pride*. Assess, which of the animosities you consider the worst.

b) **Pair** Compare your findings with a partner.

c) **Share** Discuss in class. Comment on how you would have coped in that situation if you had been that character.

LGSM and Miners: more similarities or more differences?

10

Re-watch the scene after the first demo: the foundation of LGSM and the search for miner donation acceptors (07:25 - 10:05). Find comparison parameters and compare the situation of gay and lesbian people with that of the miners.

comparison parameters	gays & lesbians	miners

Singing and dancing creates a sense of community

11

a) Read the info box.

Info

Why we dance

Making music and dancing are things that bring people together on a very deep and non verbal level. Most people really enjoy moving rhythmically to music. No wonder: the feeling for dancing is innate (= inborn) in us humans – no animal dances! If we look at the evolutionary history of humankind, it is factually assumed that people discovered music when they began to live in groups about two million years ago. This is because dancing together and making music unites people – from young to old. Moving together promotes a sense of community and is fun.

Jonathan and Hefina on the dancefloor

b) **Group A** Re-watch the scene where Jonathan dances in the miners' community hall (38:50 - 41:55) and analyse how the scene contributes to bringing the miners and the LGSM group closer together.

→ **S16** Analysis of a film scene → **Revisiting Cinematography,** pp. 103-104

Group B Re-watch the scene where the women start singing the song "Bread & Roses" (54:10 - 55:55) and analyse how this scene, the characters' behaviour, and the content of the song contribute to bringing the miners and the LGSM group closer together.

c) CHALLENGE

Discuss the significance of singing, dancing, and music throughout the film. Re-watch the following scenes:

- LGSM celebrating the final donation acceptance (14.20 - 14.30)
- LGSM's first trip to Wales (24:00 - 24:35)
- Jonathan's dance in the miners' community hall (38:50 - 41:53)
- miner women singing "Bread & Roses" (54:10 - 55:55)
- Carl dancing with a woman in Dai's living room (57:14 - 57:34)
- benefit concert at the Electric Ball Room (1:11:37 - 1:14:40)
- going clubbing: clubbing after the charity concert (1:16:15 - 1:18:02)
- end of the strike march in Onllwyn (1:34:55 - 1:36:04)
- LGSM and the miners marching together (1:49:20 - 1:52:55)

"Bread and Roses"
by James A. Oppenheim

As we go marching, marching, in the beauty of the day,
A million darkened kitchens, a thousand mill lofts gray,
Are touched with all the radiance[1] that a sudden sun discloses,
For the people hear us singing: "Bread and roses! Bread and roses!"

As we go marching, marching, we battle too for men,
For they are women's children, and we mother them again.
Our days shall not be sweated from birth until life closes;
Hearts starve as well as bodies;
give us bread, but give us roses!

As we go marching, marching, unnumbered women dead
Go crying through our singing their ancient call for bread.
Small art and love and beauty their trudging[2] spirits knew.
Yes, it is bread we fight for, but we fight for roses, too! [...]

Annotations

[1] **radiance** = warm light shining from sth
[2] **trudge** = to walk or march steadily and usually laboriously

Info

The different forms of sound in a film

- **diegetic:** sounds from 'the world inside' the film, e.g. conversation, window closing, footsteps etc.
- **non-diegetic:** sounds from 'the world outside' the film, e.g. film music, sounds creating suspense
- **voice-over (off-camera commentary):** non-diegetic information by a narrator
- **functions:**
  - to build up suspense
  - to show a certain mood / create a certain atmosphere
  - to describe a character
  - to foreshadow an event

Language support

Talking about music / sound

- The music is upbeat / gloomy / aggressive / slow / fast-paced ...
- The rhythmic / background music contributes to the atmosphere of ...
- The effect of this scene is enhanced by the music / contributes to the mood / atmosphere of the scene.
- The music provides an extra feeling of tension / adds to the atmosphere.
- The scene is accompanied by soft / alarming / melancholic music.
- The lyrics suggest ...

A shut mouth catches no flies – focus on speeches

12

Dai (17:28 - 18:58) at a gay bar and Mark (53:20 - 54:00) during his second visit around Christmas at the miners' community hall deliver central speeches that bring the miners and the lesbians & gays closer together.

a) Watch the two scenes again.

b) Analyse the speeches. → **S14** How to analyse a speech

c) Compare Dai's and Mark's speech.
- Which stylistic devices or strategies do Dai and Mark use to convince their audience?

d) **Pair work** State which speech you consider more convincing and give reasons.
→ **Langugage support** Comparing, p. 16

Help box

Stylistic devices and strategies: the use of

1. ... pictorial examples,
2. ... facts as arguments,
3. ... words with positive connotations,
4. ... the personal pronoun "we",
5. ... repetition of central words,
6. ... parallelisms (two or more sentences with a similar syntax),
7. ... anaphora (the repetition of at least two words at the beginning of two parallelly arranged sentences),
8. ... appeals,
9. ... imagery language (metaphors, similes, personifications),
10. ... contrasts,
11. ... enumerations (the listing of words or phrases, if three words / reasons are listed together, it is an example of 'rule of three'),
12. ... jokes and
13. ... unexpected turnarounds.

Dai's speech

Right then. I've had a lot of new experiences during this strike. Speaking in public. Standing on a picket line. And now I'm in a gay bar. [...]
As a matter of fact I do like it. Beer's a bit expensive, mind. But really – there's only one difference between this and a bar in South Wales. The women. They're a lot more feminine in here. But what I'm here to say to you tonight – and don't worry, it won't take long – is thank you. If you're one of the people who's put money into these buckets - if you've supported LGSM – thank you. Because what you've given us is more than money. It's friendship. And when you're in a fight as bitter and as important as this one, against an enemy, so much bigger, so much stronger than you - well. To find out that you have a friend you never knew existed - It's the best thing in the world.

notes

Mark's speech

Listen to me, everyone. I just want to say something – [...]
We've let you down. We have. We haven't collected enough. We haven't raised enough awareness - we know that. It's not enough to always be defending, sometimes you have to attack – to push forward. And that's exactly what we're going to do. When we get back to London – and you have my word on this – we are going to do something so spectacular. Alright, I'm not exactly sure what – but it'll be so incredible, so effective, that the National Coal Board – I promise you this – will come crawling on their hands and knees, in full drag, to beg you for forgiveness! Victory! Victory to the miners!

notes

d) CHALLENGE
Maureen's reservations towards LGSM and her homophobic sentiment are obvious. Imagine she had not only manipulated the further LGSM support (e.g., promoting the publishing of a negative tabloid article, bringing forward the important Union meeting to vote against the further support of the LGSM) but that she also delivered a speech at that Union meeting to make her point clear and to convince the Union members. Imagine you are Maureen and write that speech.

Language support

How to write a speech

introduction
✓ Name the speaker and, if relevant, his/her position.
✓ Say when, on what occasion and to whom the speech was delivered.
✓ Identify the theme / topic.
✓ Specify the purpose of the speech (briefly).

main body
✓ Outline the structure of the speech.
✓ Summarize the speaker's main arguments.
✓ Quote examples of stylistic devices and strategies employed by the speaker and explain their function.

conclusion
✓ Sum up your conclusions.
✓ If necessary, put the speech into its historical context.
✓ Depending on the task, give your personal opinion on whether the speech succeeds in fulfilling the speaker's objectives.

- The speaker delivers / gives / makes a speech ... / draws his attention to ... / informs about .../ appeals to feelings and emotions by ... / intends to ...
- In order to convince / persuade the audience / the listeners of his opinion, the speaker makes use of ...
- The speaker employs / makes use of ...
- By employing an ..., the speaker underlines / stresses ...
- The metaphor in line ... suggests that / illustrates that ...
- In line ... the speaker refers to / quotes ...
- The personification of ... suggests that /makes it clear that ...
- The speaker alludes to ... / suggests that ... / illustrates his argumentation by ... / compares / contrasts X with Y.

The union makes us strong

13
While dancing and delivering important speeches brings the two groups together, the symbol of shaking hands is very prominent throughout the film, too.

a) Watch the following scenes (33:14 - 33:25; 36:19 - 36:24; 1:16:15 - 1:18:02; 1:43:20 - 1:43:25; 1:48:55 - 1:49:25) again. Fill in column 1 and 2.
b) Explain what the image of shaking hands conveys in each situation (column 3).
c) Which strategies of cinematography are used to underline the image of the shaking hands (field size, camera movement / camera angle, point of view, setting / costumes)? What is the effect (column 4 and 5)? Copy the table and fill it in accordingly.

→ **Langugage support** Talking about cinematography, p. 105 → **Revisiting Cinematography,** pp. 103-104

setting	characters	reason(s) for shaking hands?	cinematic devices	effect

d) Discuss in class, to what extent this image metaphorically underlines the union that "makes them strong".

Screen duration versus plot duration

14

a) Read the text in the info box.
b) Research the common techniques mentioned to compress the plot duration.
c) Apply your gained knowledge by analysing how the plot duration is compressed in the given scenes:
   - the LGSM group returning from Onllwyn to London after their first visit and the time till Christmas (44:05 - 46:05), and
   - the time after the charity concert to the accelerated union meeting (1:17:00 - 1:23:45)

Info

Screen duration versus plot duration

Screen duration is the time that passes until a story is fully told. For a movie it is simply its length or its time duration, so for *Pride* it is 115 minutes. The time that passes within that story is called plot duration, so for example from Bromely's 20th birthday to his 21st birthday: The whole year with all events around Bromely and the LGSM (12 months = 525601minutes = plot duration) is told in 115 minutes (= screen duration). Usually a film compresses the plot duration, i.e., it is much shorter than the time span in which the story takes place. This is possible with the help of editing: Employing fades, time lapse and slow motion, the director and editor can create a new, own cinematic time beyond the possibilities of the camera within the framework of editing. Here are some examples: fade-in / fade-out, crossfade, flashback, flash-forward, jump cut, durative time-lapse, iterative time-lapse, cinematic time-lapse and music.

POST-VIEWING

A film based on a true story and real people

15 CHALLENGE

a) **Group work** Research the real people from the film *Pride* and compare the film characters with the real, authentic people and their stories.

→ **Langugage help** Talking about characters, p. 106

→ **Langugage help** Useful linking words, p. 107

- Mark Ashton
- Jonathan Blake
- Mike Jackson
- Dai Donavan
- Sian James
- Hefina Headson

Mark Ashton's bookshop – the only specificly lesbian / gay bookshop in the UK

Tip For your research you can watch the featurette on the DVD or the shorter report from the *BBC One Show*. In addition you can read the article from the *Guardian*. You can find the links here: **Webcode** DSW-73685-14

b) **Pair work** Imagine you could interview the real people.
   - What questions would you ask?
   - Based on your research, what would they answer?
   - Write down your interview and present it to the class.

Info

To **tolerate** means to have a fair and objective attitude towards people that differ from you in terms of sexual orientation, religious beliefs, nationality, race etc. You neither want to harm them nor be close friends with them. Tolerance can be seen as the most basic step to a functional society as it implies that you can live with a certain circumstance.

To **accept** goes one step further and needs tolerance as a basis. It means to welcome or even endorse the reality of differences without having any endeavors to modify it. Thus, you cannot only live with a certain circumstance, but you even judge it favourably.

Tolerance versus acceptance

16

a) Sum up which initial obstacles prevent the LGSM from supporting the miners and vice versa.
b) How are these obstacles overcome by both communities?
c) Read the info box on tolerance versus acceptance.

d) For each of the characters listed below draw developmental lines with which you show when / in which situation they reject, tolerate or accept the LGSM group. Support your ideas with striking examples (e.g., key scenes). Copy the diagram and fill it in accordingly.

Characters

- Maureen (widow and Cliff's sister-in-law)
- Lee & Johnny (Maureen's sons)
- Cliff (Maureen's brother-in-law, retired miner, union secretary)
- Carl (cubby blond miner who learns how to dance to have better chances with women)
- Gwen (elderly lady who is recently involved with vegan dishes)
- Martin (miner, Sian's husband)
- Dai (miner, who is driven by the principle of loyalty)
- Hefina (a good natured villager and strong leader in the mining community)

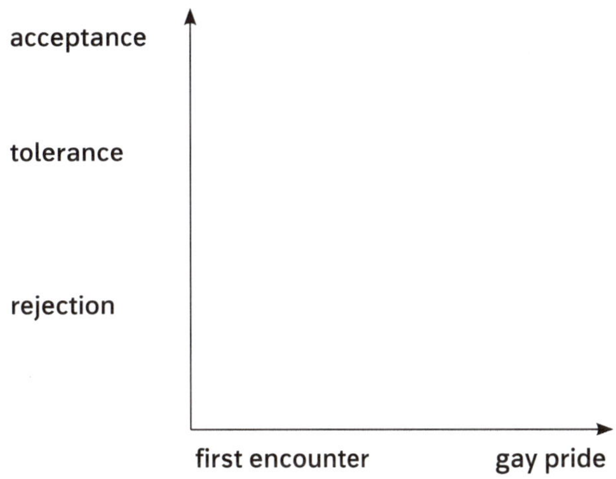

MEDIATION

17 → **S19** How to improve your mediation skills

During the miners' strike in 1984, a tabloid press article stated, "Perverts support the pits." To celebrate the support of the LGSM nearly 40 years later, you want to portray the other side of the coin and write a blog post, titled "Miners became LGBTQ Allies!", which shall be posted on the LGBTQ Nation blog.
Read the German text "Was ist ein Ally?" and use the given information to write the blog post, in which you explain what an ally is and what one can do to become a good ally. Furthermore state in how far the miners became allies to the LGBTQ community in 1985. Illustrate your arguments with examples from the film *Pride*.

→ **S7** Writing a blog post

WAS IST EIN ALLY?

Salomé Kofler

Gerade im Zusammenhang mit der #blacklivesmatter-Bewegung ist der Begriff Ally in letzter Zeit immer wieder gefallen. Aber auch in der LGBTQA+-Community kennt man den Begriff. Aber woher kommt der Begriff eigentlich und was heißt er denn jetzt ganz genau? Denn hinter dem Wort „Ally" steckt viel mehr als nur ein*e Verbündete*r.

WAS IST DENN NUN EIN ALLY?

Der Begriff Ally kommt aus dem Englischen und bedeutet direkt übersetzt so viel wie „Verbündete*r". Damit sind Menschen gemeint, die ihre Privilegien nutzen, um Minderheiten zu unterstützen. Sie verbünden sich also mit einer diskriminierten Gruppe, obwohl sie selbst kein Teil davon sind. Bekannt ist der Begriff vor allem in der LGBTQA+ Szene und durch die #blacklivesmatter-Bewegung. Ein Ally der LGBTQA+-Community nutzt zum Beispiel seine vorteilhaftere Position als hetero- und cisnormatives Individuum, um anderen Geschlechtsidentitäten zu helfen, in der Gesellschaft anerkannt zu werden.

WER KANN EIN ALLY SEIN?

Prinzipiell kann jede*r, der*die möchte und genug Bereitschaft zeigt, ein Ally sein. Allerdings geht es eben darum, diskriminierte Gruppen aktiv zu unterstützen, nur darüber zu reden, dass Unterdrückung falsch ist, reicht nicht. Um ein Ally zu sein, kann man logischerweise auch nicht selbst zur diskriminierten Gruppe gehören, mit der man sich verbünden möchte. In der Regel besitzt man eine vorteilhaftere Position in der Gesellschaft, die man gegen Ungerechtigkeit einsetzt.

WAS GENAU MACHT EIN ALLY?

Verständnis und Mitleid zeigen ist schön und wichtig, das allein macht einen Ally allerdings noch nicht aus. Es ist ausschlaggebend, dass von selbst die Initiative ergriffen wird, um eine Minderheit zu unterstützen. Man kämpft den Kampf gegen die Ungerechtigkeit, als ob es sein eigener wäre. Aktiv statt passiv sein ist also ein wichtiger Punkt. Ein Ally setzt sich nicht nur für Gerechtigkeit ein, sondern akzeptiert, dass er*sie als privilegierte Mehrheit ein Teil des Problems sein kann und geht bewusst dagegen vor, indem er*sie diese Privilegien nutzt, um Menschen mit einer schwächeren Position zu helfen. Privilegiert sein heißt in dem Fall übrigens nicht, besonders reich zu sein oder ein einfaches Leben zu haben, sondern eine bestimmte Art von Benachteiligung aufgrund struktureller Ungleichheiten nie zu erleben. Ein Ally setzt sich regelmäßig mit aktuellen Themen auseinander und bleibt so gesellschaftskritisch.

WIE KANNST DU EIN GUTER ALLY WERDEN?

Um ein guter Ally zu sein, muss man bereit sein, mit anderen und für andere zu handeln, um Unterdrückung endgültig zu beenden und Gleichheit zu schaffen. Für einen guten Ally gibt es einige Richtlinien, an die man sich halten kann. Zum einen sollte man sich über verschiedene Identitäten und Erfahrungen weiterbilden, die marginalisierte Gruppen gemacht haben (können). Zum anderen sollte man sich seine eigenen Vorurteile immer wieder bewusst machen und auch unangenehme Erkenntnisse reflektieren, um gegen unterbewusste und diskriminierende Ansichten vorgehen zu können. Aktives Engagement gegen Benachteiligung und Ungleichheit sind unerlässlich. Das heißt eben nicht nur, dagegen zu reden, wenn sich jemand rassistisch oder homophob äußert, sondern auch ohne Anstoß von außen selbst Dinge in die Hand zu nehmen. Man muss bereit sein, große persönliche, aber auch soziale, institutionelle und gesellschaftliche Veränderungen zu schaffen. Wer sich noch mehr über Allyship informieren möchte, findet hier im Übrigen einen ausführlichen Guide.

Perspectives on *Pride* – 5 minute presentations

18 CHOOSE

Diagnosis HIV / AIDS – a sure death?

Mark and Jonathan are both diagnosed positive with HIV. However, while we get to know that Mark died at a very young age, Jonathan, "number 2", celebrated his 65th birthday in 2014 when the film *Pride* was released. Throughout the film, posters warn "Tested? Aids kills."

Do some research and prepare a leaflet that explains ...

- how Aids was reported at the time of the film,
- the difference between HIV and Aids,
- possible ways of infection, precautions, medication,
- some facts and numbers,
- today's situation when being diagnosed with HIV.

OR

Power to the women – empowered female characters?

How does the film treat its different female characters? In what ways are they shown to be empowered?

OR

First rule "nobody collects alone" – violence against the LGBTQ community

The first rule of LGSM states that nobody collects alone. Later the viewers get to know the reason for the rule: Gethin was hospitalized. He was beaten up by a homophobic man.

- Do some research on "gay bashing".
- Explain what it means and how many incidents like this happen in the UK / Germany ... per year.
- Present possible measures to prevent gay bashing.

OR

Outing – "Yes, I'm gay."

Exposing yourself as lesbian, gay, bisexual, transgender etc. to others can have serious consequences on your private and work life. In *Pride* Bromely / Joe is outed and Cliff outs himself as being gay.

- Compare the different reactions.
- Try to explain the differences.

Language support

Giving a presentation

introduction	body	conclusion
• I will begin by describing / explaining ... and continue with ... Finally, I will ... • I'm going to take a look at / examine ... • The issues I want to mention / discuss ... • There are a number of things to consider when looking at the issue of ... • Have you ever thought / been in a situation where ... • You are certainly aware ... / As you know ...	• First of all, I will ... and then I will go on to ... Then / next ... / Finally / Lastly ... • To begin with I'd like to say a few things about ... • In addition ... • Let's consider this in more detail. ... • This leads me to my next point ... • A good example of this is ... • As an illustration, ... • To give you an example ... • To illustrate this point ... • In other words ... / So, what I am saying is ...	• So, what we have learned today is ... / To summarize, the most important points are ... • I would like now to recap ... • I think it is fair to say ... • I'd like to stress / highlight / emphasize the following points ... • I am happy to answer any queries / questions ... • If you would like me to elaborate on any point, please ask.

Review

19

After having dealt with Matthew Warchus' film *Pride* in detail, write a film review for an online audience.

Checklist

How to write a film review

A film review offers information on a film. It is usually a recommendation for a film or informs its readers why it might not be worth watching.

✓ Start with a catchy introduction in which you give essential information about the film (title, director, genre, release date, actors, characters, setting and plot).
✓ Then, give a brief summary of what the film is about, but avoid spoilers.
✓ Afterwards, state your personal impression of the film.
✓ Finally, point out the purpose of the film and come up with a convincing conclusion as to why the reader should or should not watch the film.

Language support

Writing a film review

How to start:
- The film "..." is a drama / a comedy / an action film (...)
- The film was directed / produced by ... and released in ... / The film was-well directed by ...
- Starring ... (actor's name) / The main character is played ... / ... is absolutely remarkable as ...
- The film won ... / was awarded ...

Characters / plot:
- The main character is called ...
- The story is about / deals with / focusses on ...
- The film tells the story of ...
- As the story continues / unfolds / develops ...
- The plot is multi-dimensional / complicated / thrilling / captivating / arouses curiosity / is full of tension ...
- The plot hast a surprising twist.
- One of the best moments in the film is when ...
- The characters are believable / shallow / unconvincing ...

Setting:
- It is set in ...
- The story takes place in / unfolds in ...
- The film begins in ...
- The film creates a ... atmosphere / mood ...

Cinematography:
- The camera work is impressive / spectacular / unrealistic / confusing
- The camera operations draw attention to ...
- The special effects are stunning / impressive / poor / amateurish.
- The music is profound / clichéd / conveys a ... atmosphere ...
- The music underlines emotions / connects scenes.

Opinion:
- I believe ...
- I (highly / strongly / definitely) recommend / don't recommend this film because ...
- A 'must-see' / box-office success / failure. / Don't miss it!
- A very impressive portrayal of ...
- From 1-10, I give this film a ...
- If you like ... this film is for you.
- The film is a worthwhile watch. / I'm afraid the film is a complete waste of time and money. Only watch this film if you have plenty of time to spare.
- ... is well worth seeing / not to be missed / a truly great piece of filmmaking.
- The film is thought-provoking / touching / moving.

Stereotypes, clichés and prejudices: definitions

1

Every day, people of different ethnic or social groups experience discrimination in various forms and facets. Being treated unequally is also a major theme in Matthew Warchus' film *Pride*.

Info

- A **stereotype** is an opinion that can be adopted about specific types of individuals or certain ways of doing things. These thoughts or beliefs may or may not accurately reflect reality.
- You can differentiate between:
  - an **autostereotype**, which is an opinion that one group forms about itself. The autostereotype is often more differentiated than the heterostereotype. The positive attributes are dominating.
  - a **heterostereotype**, which is more an association, a prejudice used by a group to define others. The heterostereotype is tending to the black-or-white pattern: showing stronger generalization or simplification.
- A **prejudice** is an unfair and unreasonable opinion or feeling, especially when formed without enough thought or knowledge.
- A **cliché** is a popular or common saying or remark that has lost originality and ingenuity by long overuse.

a) Using your knowledge from the info box above, decide whether the following sentences are a stereotype (auto- or hetero), prejudice (often negative heterostereotypes) or a cliché. Draw lines.

• autostereotypes	Some foreigners believe that all "Germans are Nazis or fascists."
• heterostereotypes	A queer woman states: "Homosexuals are good lovers."
• prejudice	A German friend of mine states: "All Latinos dance well."
• cliché	"All gay men are hairdressers."

b) Have you ever been confronted with stereotypes and / or prejudices?
CHOOSE
If so, how did you feel? What did you do?
OR
If not, can you imagine how people might feel when being valued solely on the basis of stereotypes and prejudices?

c) Outline examples of autostereotypes, heterostereotypes and prejudices in *Pride* and refer to specific incidences / scenes.

d) **Pair work** Movie directors often work with clichés to insert some humour and hidden critique in the plot line. Did you recognize any clichés in the film? Take notes.

e) **Pair work** In your opinion, what might be the reason for including obvious clichés in a film dealing with discrimination?

f) Write a formal letter to the script writer / director, in which you summarize your findings on clichés in *Pride*. State your opinion and ask for clarification. → **S3** Checklist: Formal letter

An overview of the different forms of discrimination

2

a) In order to raise awareness for discriminatory practices in everyday life, read the article "Forms of discrimination."

b) Prepare an infographic, in which you …
- define discrimination,
- describe possible forms of discrimination, and
- state the consequences of discrimination.

Tip You may use free software tools like canva.com to create your infographic!

Checklist

Infographic

An infographic is a concise visualization of a subject's most important facts on one single page using headings, bullet points and / or images and tables. Effective infographics split the information into different sections (cf. ideas). The following guideline will help you.

✓ Organize your research well.
✓ Make a simple outline.
✓ Think of great header information.
✓ Design or choose an infographic template.
✓ Concisely add the facts.
✓ Publish and present your infographic.

c) **Pair work** Examine which forms of discrimination can be found in *Pride*. Illustrate your findings with key scenes.

Forms of discrimination

Discrimination strikes at the very heart of being human. It is harming someone's rights simply because of who they are or what they believe. Discrimination is harmful and perpetuates[1] inequality.

We all have the right to be treated equally, regardless of our race, ethnicity[2], nationality, class, […], religion, belief, sex, gender, language, sexual orientation, gender identity, sex characteristics, age, health or other status. Yet all too often we hear heartbreaking stories of people who suffer cruelty simply for belonging to a "different" group from those in positions of privilege or power.

Discrimination occurs when a person is unable to enjoy his or her human rights or other legal rights on an equal basis with others because of an unjustified distinction made in policy[3], law or treatment. […]

Discrimination can take various forms:

Direct discrimination is when an explicit distinction is made between groups of people that results in individuals from some groups being less able than others to exercise their rights. For example, a law that requires women, and not men, to provide proof of a certain level of education as a prerequisite[4] for voting would constitute direct discrimination on the grounds of sex.

Indirect discrimination is when a law, policy, or practice is presented in neutral terms (that is, no explicit distinctions are made) but it disproportionately disadvantages a specific group or groups. For example, a law that requires everyone to provide proof of a certain level of education as a prerequisite for voting has an indirectly discriminatory effect on any group that is less likely to have achieved that level of education (such as disadvantaged ethnic groups or women).

Intersectional discrimination is when several forms of discrimination combine to leave a particular group or groups at an even greater disadvantage. For example, discrimination against women frequently means that they are paid less than men for the same work. Discrimination against an ethnic minority often results in members of that group being paid less than others for the same work. Where women from a minority group are paid less than other women and less than men from the same minority group, they are suffering from intersectional discrimination on the grounds of their sex, gender and ethnicity. […]

Annotations
[1] to **perpetuate** = to make sth such as a bad situation, belief, etc. continue for a long time
[2] **ethnicity** = a particular ethnic affiliation or group
[3] **policy** = a plan of action agreed or chosen by a political party
[4] **prerequisite** = sth must exist or happen before sth else can happen or be done

WHAT DRIVES DISCRIMINATION?
At the heart of all forms of discrimination is prejudice based on concepts of identity, and the need to identify with a certain group. This can lead to division, hatred and even the dehumanization of other people because they have a different identity. In many parts of the world, the politics of blame and fear is on the rise. Intolerance, hatred and discrimination is causing an ever-widening rift[5] in societies. [...]

SOME KEY FORMS OF DISCRIMINATION
Racial and ethnic discrimination
Racism affects virtually every country in the world. It systematically denies people their full human rights just because of their colour, race, ethnicity, descent[6] [...] or national origin. Racism unchecked can fuel large-scale atrocities[7] such as the 1994 genocide[8] in Rwanda and more recently, apartheid and ethnic cleansing of the Rohingya people in Myanmar. [...]

Discrimination against non-nationals, sometimes known as xenophobia
Discrimination against non-nationals is frequently based on racism or notions of superiority [...]. Since 2008, **South Africa** has experienced several outbreaks of violence against refugees, asylum seekers and migrants from other African countries, including killings, and looting or burning of shops and businesses. In some instances, the violence has been inflamed by the hate-filled rhetoric of politicians who have wrongly labelled foreign nationals "criminals" and accused them of burdening the health system.
Discrimination has also been a feature of the response of authorities to refugees and asylum seekers in other parts of the world. Many people in countries receiving refugees and asylum-seekers view the situation as a crisis with leaders and politicians exploiting these fears by promising, and in some cases enacting, abusive and unlawful policies.
For example, **Hungary passed a package of punitive[9] laws in 2018**, which target groups that the government has identified as supporting refugees and migrants. The authorities have also subjected refugees and asylum seekers to violent push-backs and ill-treatment and imposed arbitrary[10] detention[11] on those attempting to enter Hungarian territory. [...]

Discrimination against lesbian, gay, bisexual, transgender and intersex (LGBTI) people
Everywhere in the world, people face discrimination because of who they love, who they are attracted to and who they are. Lesbian, gay, bisexual, transgender and intersex (LGBTI) people risk being unfairly treated in all areas of their lives, whether it's in education, employment, housing or access to health care, and they may face harassment and violence.
Some countries punish people for their sexual orientation or their gender identity with jail or even death. For example, in October 2019, Uganda's Ethics and Integrity Minister announced that the government was planning to introduce the **death penalty** for consensual same-sex sexual acts. [...] It is extremely difficult, and in most cases, impossible for LGBTI people to live their lives freely and seek justice for abuses when the laws are not on their side. Even when they are, there is strong stigma and stereotyping of LGBTI identities that prevents them from living their lives as equal members of society or accessing rights and freedoms that are available to others. That's why LGBTI activists campaign relentlessly for their rights: whether it's to be free from discrimination to love who they want, have **their gender legally recognized** or to just be protected from the risk of assault and harassment. [...]

Gender discrimination
In many countries, in all regions of the world, laws, policies, customs and beliefs exist that deny women and girls their rights.
By law, women cannot dress as they like (Saudi Arabia, Iran) or work at night (Madagascar) or take out a loan without their husband's signature (Equatorial Guinea). In many countries, discriminatory laws place limits on a woman's right to divorce, own property, exercise control over her

Annotations
[5] **rift** = division; a serious break in the relationship between people
[6] **descent** = a person's family origins
[7] **atrocity** = a cruel and violent act, especially in a war
[8] **genocide** = the murder of a large number of people from a particular nation or ethnic group, with the aim of destroying that nation or group
[9] **punitive** = intended as punishment
[10] **arbitrary** = not seeming to be based on a reason, system or plan and sometimes seeming unfair
[11] **detention** = the state of being kept in a place

own body and enjoy protection from harassment. In the ongoing battle for justice, hundreds of thousands of women and girls take to the streets to claim their human rights and demand gender equality. In the USA, Europe and Japan, women protested against misogyny[12] and abuse as part of the #MeToo marches. In Argentina, Ireland and Poland, women demonstrated to demand a stop to oppressive abortion laws. In Saudi Arabia, they called for an end to the driving ban, and in Iran, they demanded an end to forced *hijab* (veiling[13]). All over the world, women and girls have been at the forefront of demands for change.

Yet despite the stratospheric rise of women's activism, the stark reality remains that many governments around the world openly support policies, laws and customs that subjugate[14] and suppress women. [...]

Discrimination based on disability

As many as 1 in 10 people around the world lives with a disability. Yet in many societies, people with disabilities must grapple with stigma, being ostracized[15] and treated as objects of pity or fear. Developing countries are home to about 80 per cent of people with disabilities. The overwhelming majority of people with disabilities – 82 per cent – live below the poverty line. Women with disabilities are two to three times more likely to encounter physical and sexual abuse than women without disabilities.

In **Kazakhstan**, current laws mean that thousands of people with psychosocial and intellectual disabilities have been declared "incapable" by law and put in the care of a guardian. Under this system they cannot exercise their rights and are not able to challenge the decision in court. [...]

Annotations

[12] **misogyny** = a feeling of hate or dislike towards women, or a feeling that women are not as good as men

[13] **veiling** = to cover sth with sth in a way that hides it partly or completely

[14] to **subjugate** = to gain control over sb / sth

[15] **ostracized** = excluded

Love is love: terms / concepts with regard to sexual diversity

3

a) Love comes in many forms and facets. For a long time, there was talk of LGBTQ+. This acronym has now been extended. Match each term with its suitable description.

	term	letter	description	result
1.	lesbian	a	... describes the lack of sexual attraction or desire for other people.	1.
2.	gay	b	... refers to people identifying and / or presenting themselves as neither distinguishably masculine nor feminine.	2.
3.	bisexual	c	... describes a woman who is emotionally, romantically, or sexually attracted to other women.	3.
4.	transgender	d	... describes a person who is emotionally, romantically, or sexually attracted to more than one sex, gender or gender identity though not necessarily simultaneously, in the same way or to the same degree.	4.
5.	queer	e	... describes a person who is emotionally, romantically, or sexually attracted to members of the same gender.	5.
6.	androgynous	f	... is seen as an umbrella term for people whose gender identity and / or expression is different from cultural expectations based on the sex they were assigned at birth. However, it does not imply any specific sexual orientation.	6.
7.	asexual	g	... is a term people often use to express fluid identities and orientations.	7.
8.	non-binary	h	...describes a person who does not identify exclusively as a man or a woman. They may identify as being both a man and a woman, somewhere in between, or as falling completely outside these categories.	8.

b) In the table from a) you see the many facets of sexual diversity. Which aspects are considered / displayed in the film *Pride*?
c) Based on your findings, do you consider LGSM a sexually diverse group? Why (not)?
d) **Group work (3-4)** Think about the depiction of sexuality in *Pride*. Describe some key scenes that you would relate to portrayals of sexuality.
e) **Pair work** Imagine you could talk to the script writer / director: You confront him / her with your findings regarding sexual diversity and sexuality in *Pride*. He / she gives arguments, defending his / her portrayals of sexual diversity and sexuality in *Pride*.
   - Each of you takes notes for one side.
   - Then initiate a debate.

Gay Pride

4 Think–Pair–Share

a) **Think** What could gay Pride Parade and its history be about? State your ideas.

____

____

b) **Pair** Compare your ideas.
c) **Share** Present your ideas to the class.

LISTENING

5

a) Take a close look at the following infographic.
b) Listen twice to Peter Tatchell, a gay rights activist, explaining the history of the LGBTQ+ pride march. You can find a link to the video here: **Webcode** DSW-73685-15. Complete the box with keywords while listening. The bullet points indicate the number of aspects.

Peter Tatchell

1. 	date and approximate number of participants of the very first gay pride parade in Britain:	• •
2. 	reasons why members of the gay community had reservations or even fear of attending the very first gay pride parade:	• •
3. 	reaction by the public during the parade:	• • • •

4. 	number of police officers on duty, their actions and reasons for their behaviour during the parade:	• • • •
5. 	location of the end of the very first gay pride parade and actions of the marchers:	• • •
6. 	reasons for behaviour in public in defiance and police's reaction:	• •
7. 	number of gay pride parade participants in the following years until 1987:	•
8. 	reasons why 1988 was a milestone for gay pride and its movement:	• • •
9. 	examples of homophobic violence in Britain and around the world:	• • •

c) Bromley / Joe experiences the Gay Pride Parade at the beginning and at the end of the film *Pride* (scenes: 00:02:50 - 00:04:20 and 01:49:25 - 01:52:06).
Compare the two scenes (e.g. with regard to Bromley's behaviour, reactions etc.).

d) Then analyse in how far the two scenes wrap up Bromley's development.

e) CHALLENGE
Use Peter Tatchell's information on the history of the LGBTQ+ pride march and do additional research on the internet about the gay rights movement in England. Focus on the rights of the gay community then and now. Present your information in a digitally created infographic and present it.
→ **Checklist** Infographic, p. 118

Crisis of adolescence? Coming of age

6

a) Read the following informative text about growing up and the coming-of-age genre.

b) Transfer the given pieces of information into a suitable graphic organizer (e.g., mind / concept map, flow chart, plot diagram, fish-bone graphic etc.).

c) Examine in how far the film *Pride* can be seen as a coming-of-age story by focusing on and exemplifying Bromley's (i.e. Joe Cooper's) and Gethin Robert's development. Use your graphic organizer and add information in different colours.

The Crises of Adolescence

The transition between childhood and adulthood, becoming an adult or entering maturity, is referred to as 'coming of age'.

Coming-of-age as a genre refers to literature and films in which older children and adolescents[1] encounter[2] fundamental issues of growing up or intense emotions that call for maturing[3] socially and psychologically for the first time. The focus is on the confrontation with the adult world, the parental home, school, and society. The plot usually revolves around family, social, or individual conflicts, sexuality, gender roles, rebellion, opinion formation, and other moral as well as emotional challenges that young people face during puberty. The protagonist will encounter loss or discovery, or an internal or external conflict, making him or her suffer from arduous[4] trials and misfortunes and personal development, change, and growth. However, these crucial[5] experiences will eventually lead to life-altering adulthood despite scarification[6]. The protagonist will find him- or herself clashing with their traditional culture and societal standards while progressing. Courses of self-discovery, identity formation, and emancipation are characteristic of this genre. It is the protagonist's psychological or sometimes even physical journey from being a child to being an adult: from naïve to wise, from idealist to realist, and from immature to mature. Dialogues and emotional responses are more in focus than the action itself. Often the story is told in the form of flashbacks. Both provide deep insights into the protagonist.

The typical plot pattern of a coming-of-age story is as follows: At the beginning, the exposition, the protagonist is in a childhood stage. He or she is young, naïve, and feels alienated[7] and alone. As his or her story proceeds, the action rises to a conflict. Here the protagonist encounters a challenge or a problem. The plot continues with the protagonist's struggle to overcome this challenge. At one turning point, comparable to a climax, there is a sudden realization of the truth about him- or herself or the word, a so-called epiphany[8]. The protagonist makes a tough decision regarding his / her problem and starts changing because of this decision. With falling action comes the story's conclusion, in which the protagonist displays evidence of change. He / she has found a sense of belonging or self-realization reaching maturity. He or she is now seen as different and the significance of the change is revealed. The protagonist finally enters the adulthood stage.

Because of the universal, relatable and dramatic nature of these coming-of-age narrative motifs, the genre is the most popular one of literacy fiction. Mark Twain's *The Adventures of Tom Sawyer*, the *Harry Potter* series by J.K. Rowling, or Stephenie Meyer's *Twilight*, are some prominent examples.

Annotations

[1] **adolescent** = a young person who is developing from a child into an adult
[2] to **encounter** = to come upon or experience especially unexpectedly
[3] to **mature** = to develop emotionally and start to behave like a sensible adult
[4] **arduous** = involving a lot of effort and energy, especially over a period of time
[5] **crucial** = vital, important
[6] **scarification** = the giving up of sth for sth better, or for a good moral reason
[7] **alienated** = feeling of not belonging
[8] **epiphany** = a sudden and surprising moment of understanding

7

a) CHOOSE

Write a diary entry: After a turbulent year and his forced coming out, Bromely / Joe decides to start writing a diary. Imagine you are Bromeley / Joe! Write his first diary entry reflecting upon his coming-of-age story.

OR

Write a dialogue: Encouraged by his new positive experience in his native Wales and also reinforced by Hefina's advocacy, Gethin decides to visit his mother, with whom he has had no contact for many years. The film shows their first meeting, but what Gethin and his mother discuss remains hidden from the viewer. Assume you are the script writer, develop and write a dialogue focusing on their first encounter.

→ **Checklist** p. 69

Checklist

Writing a diary entry

- ✓ start with "Dear Diary,"
- ✓ write in the first person,
- ✓ be honest and reflective,
- ✓ reflect on and express your feelings.

b) Read out your diary entry or practice your dialogue with a partner and act it out.

8 CHALLENGE

a) **Pair work** Discuss with a partner if *Pride* can be classified as a coming-of-age story.

b) Write an argumentative essay, in which you examine why *Pride* can be classified as a coming-of-age story. → **S6** How to write a discussion / comment

PRE-READING

1

Read the title and the PREMEDIATION. Speculate on what the play will be about.

2

a) Read the article about the dramatist Jasmine Lee-Jones.
b) Find out more about her:
- age
- family background
- motivation for writing the play
- ideals
- personal experiences with theatre
- ...

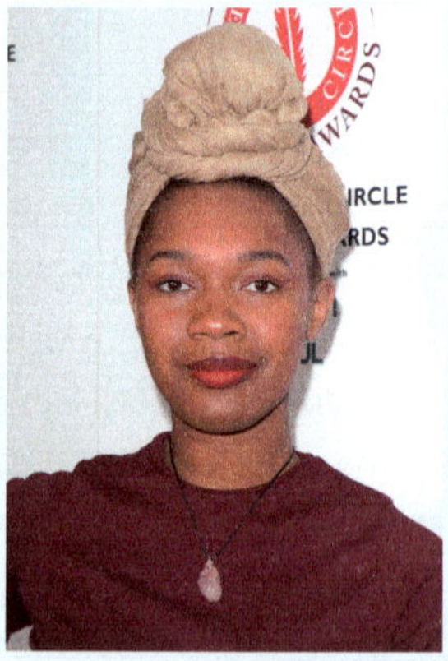

Jasmine Lee-Jones interview: I want people to come to the theatre like they watch Netflix

by Jessie Thompson

[...] Jasmine Lee-Jones's debut play, exploring female friendship, cultural appropriation and the internet, became one of the most talked-about plays of the year after a triumphant run at the Royal Court, picking up a trail of awards and an ecstatic stream of social media appreciation. [...]

It's immediately obvious when talking to Lee-Jones IRL, [...] that she is a deep and impressive thinker, often pausing for several seconds before she answers a question. [...] Born in North London, Lee-Jones became interested in theatre because of a strong connection she felt with words and language. "I always wanted to read things out loud," she says. "When I found theatre, I started to realise: oh, you can do a job where you're actually paid to speak words aloud, to really interrogate language." [...]

The play's text is written in gifs, online acronyms, merging the IRL-world with the social media-sphere. It's the most original and successful way any writer has ever managed to capture the internet on stage, but Lee-Jones didn't do it on purpose – she just wanted it to feel real. "I think theatre can sometimes feel quite isolating like, oh, this is for someone else. We have a prestige about theatre and what should be on stage, like it's just for Shakespeare. And then you put something in from the internet that feels very casual and personal to people, and people are willing to give you more license," she says.

[...] The online reaction to seven methods made it clear that the play was reaching new, more diverse audiences, something that matters greatly to Lee-Jones. "I want people to come to the theatre like they watch Netflix," she says. "I like watching reality TV and all of that as much as the next person. But one thing I find super interesting about TV is everyone will watch good, really thoroughly written, well-plotted TV. [...] But when there's something really good in theatre on, people still feel like it's not for them. There's a universality to TV and film that theatre just hasn't created yet. It's still like, oh, it's meant for those people."

Having been nurtured as a writer by the Royal Court from the age of 17, Lee-Jones has always felt more comfortable there than at other theatres. But she had an experience a few years ago that shook that. She was watching a play with a friend, also a black woman, and they were waiting at the bar to get a drink. "This group of white people, I think maybe husband and wife, just went in front of us. I looked at my friend and was like, did you see that? And she just nodded, but eventually I realised they just didn't see us. They didn't think we were there to do something important or watch a show. They thought we were kind of just loitering," she tells me. "I think that was the first experience I had in this theatre where I realised – not because of the theatre, necessarily – but there's an audience that thinks this space belongs to them more than other people."

In the post-pandemic era, Lee-Jones thinks the theatre world will only bring in new audiences if it's really committed to doing so. "They have to keep programming the plays until people feel safe enough to come to the work. And what happened to me in the bar downstairs doesn't keep happening, because people realise: oh, this space is for everyone, it's not just for us." As she's telling me this, just behind her is the Royal Court's building; on the front of it, her name is written in neon lights. How thrilling that, right now, that one belongs to her. [...]

3

Pair work State what you know about Kylie Jenner, the American media celebrity. Find out on the Internet and then decide whether the statements are true or false (if it is false, correct the statement).

	true	false	correction
1. Kylie Jenner is the daughter of Caitlyn and Kris Jenner.			
2. Kylie Jenner belongs to the generation alpha.			
3. She was part of the reality TV series “Keeping up with the Kardashians” because she was adopted by Robert Kardashian.			
4. Jenner launched her own cosmetics line called *Kylie's BW lip kit*.			
5. In 2017, Jenner was placed on the Forbes Celebrity 100 list, making her the youngest person to be featured on the list.			
6. Kylie Jenner beat Mark Zuckerberg by two years when being announced the youngest self-made billionaire in 2019.			
7. Kylie Jenner is black.			

Language

4

a) Users of social media normally don't use formal language. What abbreviations do you use?

CHOOSE

Pair work If you prefer the analogue world you may write the abbreviations down.

OR

Group work You may use the online tool on oncoo.de for this task.

b) Rewrite the following comment in Standard English.

INCOGNEGRO @INCOGNEGRO
Errybody and they aunty need to quit fronting like Kylie killing it! She ain't killing shit! And tbh if I had it my way the only thing geetting kilt would be that bitch! #kyliegjennerfidead (p. 5)

5

Reading social media content in another language can be confusing. All the slang, idioms and abbreviations people use can make even simple sentences tricky to understand.

a) Get acquainted with the abbreviations the protagonists are using by finding the correct partners: which abbreviation means what? Write the matching partners from the box into the table.

actually | Big man thing / honestly in all seriousness | Don't piss me off! | Go on! | I don't care! | Kiss my teeth! | Never mind! | Not gonna lie. | Oh my days! | Say no more! | Swear to god! | to be honest | What are you doing? | What the hell!

abbreviation	meaning
LEWL	*similar to LOL*
DPMO	
OMDS	
BMT	
IDC	
SNM	
S2g	
Nvm	
wyd	
KMT	
ngl	
acc	
WTH	
tbh	
gwarn	

b) Now compare your entries with the list of the most important abbreviations used in the play. You can find a link to the list here: **Webcode** **DSW-73685-16**

c) While reading the play add more abbreviations to the list that are used by the protagonists.

d) Rewrite the following e-mail as a tweet by using as many abbreviations as possible.

> Hello my best friend in the twitter world!
> How are you today? I can't believe we're finally meeting each other. Have I told you that my mom believes you don't exist? That's extremely funny!!!!! However, I can't wait to meet you in real life. I'll see you in Berlin next week!
> Bye for now,
> your dearest friend.

e) **CHALLENGE** You may add content to make the tweet more realistic.

f) **OPTIONAL** Rewrite the following hypothetical tweet into Standard English.

> Look @ her DP. What a QT! tbh, that's only in TL – never IRL! Check YT 4 more lies!

WHILE READING

Keeping notes

6

Tip Keeping a reading journal with the focus of summarizing the content as well as adding information about place and time and the relevant page numbers can be one option for remembering the content of a play. Taking notes with a specific focus (e.g. on one of the characters, topics, langauge etc.) is another option to structure the content of a play.

CHOOSE

Focus on one character's perspective: What aspects of Kylie's life are making Cleo furious? Take notes while reading.

OR

Focus on language: The playwright uses words from the black community, like "kiking" (p. 14) "bredrin" (p. 8) etc. Find more examples and explain their meanings.

OR

Focus on language: The play deals with serious topics but in a comical tone. Find examples from the text and evaluate the author's decision to make use of comic elements. Finally fill in your results in the following table:

quotation	topic	effect
1.		
2.		
3.		
4.		

THE PREMEDIATION (PP. 1-3)

7

a) Fill in the table.

1. **Who** are the characters?	
2. **When** do the scenes take place?	
3. **Where** does the action take place?	
4. **What** action is described?	
5. **What** references are made to the world outside the stage?	

b) In the newest version of her play from 2021, Jasmine Lee-Jones makes considerable changes to the PREMEDIATION from the original version from 2019 (see below). If you were Jasmin Lee-Jones and were asked by journalists why you made those changes to the play, apart from "A work of art is never finished" what would you answer?

The present.
In the most present sense of the present tense.
5th March 2019.
Early morning. Outside. A park. Dark.

KARA and CLEO drag something resembling a body onto the platform. They open the traps and throw it in. Cover it with earth. Suddenly they stop, standing over the body.

Blackout.

PART 1 (PP. 4-9): THE START

8

a) Cleo retweets a tweet by Forbes. Describe the "Forbes-tweet" in your own words.

____

b) Cleo is angry about the tweet's hypocrisy. Explain why.

____

c) Cleo creates the hashtag #kyliejennerfidead as a response to the Forbes tweet and tweets hypothetical death threat at Kylie Jenner. Describe Cleo's methods in your own words.

Method #1: ____

Method #2: ____

d) Complete the sentence: With tweeting the first two methods of killing, Cleo wants to point out / criticize / make aware of the facts / aim at ...

____

e) Fill in the summary with the appropriate adjectives from the box:

angry | crazy | happy | hypothetical | ingenious | real | surprise | worried

The first part of the plot describes developments in the Twitter world as well as in real life. When the action takes place in ______________ life, Cleo gets a ______________ visit from Kara. Kara had seen Cleo's tweets and wants to know why she is ______________. Cleo plays down the seriousness of her ______________________ death threats and therefore wants to calm her ______________ friend.

PART 2 (PP. 10-27): TL AND IRL

9

Social media users are responding to Cleo's tweets (pp. 10-13).

Pair work

a) List the words they are using.

b) Read the infobox. Describe the tweets' tone.

Language support

Talking about the tone

accusatory | admiring | aggressive | ambivalent | amused | appreciative | colloquial | concerned | critical | defensive | dis-/respectful | dis-/approving | judgmental ...

Info

Tone

Tone refers to an author's use of words and writing style to convey his or her attitude towards a topic. Tone is transported through diction (choice of words), viewpoint, syntax (grammar, how you put words together) and level of formality.

c) Explain the following quote in the play's context:

"Inside that tweet is hundreds of years of anti-blackness, positive affirmations of capitalism, cultural appropriation […]" (p. 15)

d) Name and describe Method #3 in your own words.

e) Describe the tone of the responses to Method #3.

f) CHOOSE

Pair work Kara and Cleo are not of the same opinion on various matters. They are having an argument about the tweets' importance (p. 15). List their arguments.

topic of discussion: "It's (just) a tweet"	
Kara	Cleo

OR
Kara and Cleo are having an argument about the application of violence as an answer to oppression (p. 21). List their arguments.

topic of discussion: "violence is the answer to oppression"	
Kara	Cleo

g) Cleo has broken up with her boyfriend. Explain why his new girlfriend upsets Cleo.

h) OPTIONAL
Pair work Act out the scene in which the two girls talk about Cleo's boyfriend, the breakup and the new girlfriend.
OR
Group work (4) Create a freeze frame in which the relationships between the following characters become apparent: Cleo, Cleo's boyfriend, the new girlfriend and Kara. You may also add up to three sentences that each character is saying.

The protagonists

10 CHOOSE
Group work What do you get to know about Cleo when reading the play? Write down her profile. Note down the pages, e.g. university student (p. 9).

Age: ______

Education: ______

Family and friends: ______

Topics of interest: ______

Political views: ______

Sexual orientation: ______

Black identity (appearance, language etc.): ______

Character traits: ______

OR
Group work What do you get to know about Kara when reading the play? Write down her profile. Note down the pages.

Age: ______

Education: ______

Family and friends: ___

Topics of interest: ___

Political views: ___

Sexual orientation: ___

Black identity (appearance, language etc.): ___

Character traits: ___

PART 3 (PP. 28-53): BACKGROUND

11

a) Name and describe Method #4 in your own words.

___

b) Describe the tone of the twitter responses to Method #4.

___

LISTENING

12

Dr. Kathomi Gatwiri, a senior Academic, psychotherapist and the founder of Healing Together Psychotherapy is talking about the term "gaslighting". You can find a link to the video here: **Webcode** DSW-73685-17

a) Listen to the first part of episode 1: "Racial gaslighting" (00:00-3:26). Decide whether the following sentences are right or wrong. Correct the statements when they are wrong.

	right	wrong	correction
1. Gaslighting is a form of physical abuse.			
2. People who are being gaslighted know that they are being manipulated and are therefore content about their knowledge.			
3. The term refers to a movie in which a husband convinces his wife that she is just imagining the dimming of lights.			
4. Racial gaslighting is when people of colour are told that their experiences are acknowledged.			
5. Racial gaslighting is deliberately used to maintain white supremacy.			
6. The more black people resist to this racial hierarchy the more acceptance they are experiencing in society.			

b) "My own bredrin gaslighting me" (p. 32). Explain Cleo's accusation.

13

Which sentences about Kara's and Cleo's past are correct? Give proof from the text. → **S23** How to quote

The primary school teachers admired Cleo's curly hair.

Cleo was always in Kara's shadow.

Cleo had many boyfriends when she was young.

Kara is satisfied with her appearance.

Cleo accuses Kara of not having helped her at a party.

14

a) Name and describe Method #5.

____

b) Describe the tweets responding to Cleo's method #5. What historical references are made? (twitterludes 4 and 5)

____

PART 4 (PP. 54-78): CHANGES

15

a) Cleo's tweets get out of hand when one of her older tweets is re-tweeted by someone else.

- What gets re-tweeted and why?

____

- How does Cleo respond?

____

b) **Pair work** Both Cleo and Kara share stories from the past to explain when they felt misunderstood by each other.

- Partner A: Outline Cleo's story of #wiggate (pp. 45-48).
- Partner B: Outline Kara's story of T'Sharn's 13th birthday party (p. 66).
- Give feedback on how well the summary was performed by your partner.

c) CHALLENGE

Comment on the following statement: "If they had acted differently in the past their relationship now would be a different one". Justify your answer.

d) Name and describe Method #6.

____

e) Put these events into the right order:

- [ ] Her identity in real life is revealed on Twitter.
- [ ] Cleo's IRL and TL identities merge into one.
- [ ] Cleo and Kara have a fight about Cleo's behaviour at T'sham's birthday party.
- [ ] Cleo is blocked from following Kara's Twitter account.
- [ ] Someone on TL re-tweets a comment by Cleo accusing her of being homophobic.
- [ ] Cleo apologizes for the two homophobic tweets from 2014.

f) In Method #7, Cleo wants Kylie Jenner to experience the same mistreatments that Saartjie must have gone through. Which mistreatments does Cleo mean? Describe the historical context Cleo is referring to.

PART 5 (PP. 79-83): THE END

16

a) With the sentence "I just don't wanna feel heavy no more" (p. 79) Cleo describes a burden she is carrying. From what burden does Cleo need to be freed?

b) Saartjie's spirit is appearing. What are Kara and Cleo praising her for?

c) The image from the PREMEDIATION of Cleo and Kara standing over a body reappears in the POST-MORTEM.

> **Info**
> The post mortem interval is the time that has elapsed since a person has died. The term can also be applied to the post mortem examination of a corpse in order to determine the cause of death.

Why do you think Jasmine Lee-Jones chose this title for the last scene?

POST-READING

Relationships

17

a) Describe the friendship between Kara and Cleo.

> **Help** Look at the following pages: 7-9, 21-25, 32-40, 48-49, 59-60, 66, 69-73, 79ff.
> Then draw a table like the one below.

section	content	description of their friendship / relationship

b) In the following quote Cleo makes a reference to slaverey on a plantation:
"Back in the old days I'd be the field nigger out shucking corn and you'd be in the house beating the master." (p. 39)
- Explain the parallels she is drawing.
- What does the quote reveal about the friendship between Cleo and Kara?

c) Kara is blocking Cleo from following @KARA and viewing her tweets. Describe Cleo's reaction. How would you feel if your best friend did that to you?

d) **Pair work** At the end of the play, Cleo and Kara share a spiritual encounter with Snaartjie.
- Does this experience strengthen their friendship?
- Discuss: Will they stay friends?

18 CHOOSE

Group work Create five freeze frames in which you show the development of Kara and Cleo's relationship. You may act between the freeze frames.

OR

Choose a part of Cleo and Kara's conversation described on the pages 32 to 35, l. 3. Act out the scene.

19

Pair work Talk for five minutes about the question in the bubble and come to a conclusion.

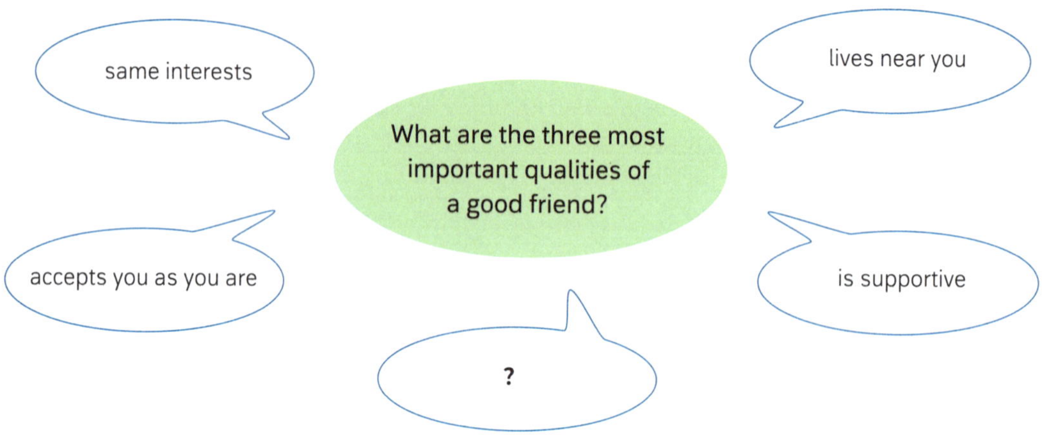

Characterization

20 CHOOSE

Write a characterization of Cleo (including her online and offline identity)

OR

Kara.

Consider if Cleo's and / or Kara's character develop throughout the play. Illustrate and proove it with the text.

→ **S23** How to quote → **Language support** Comparing, p. 16

> Tip You can find language support for writing a characterization in *Camden Town Oberstufe* on page 353.

Illustrations and graphic layout of the play's script

21

a) On social media, words are often flanked by photos, emojis, cartoons etc. Look at the following pages: 4, 10, 12, 13, 17, 44.

b) Explain the combined use of language and illustrations in TL. Draw a box like the one below and fill in your findings.
- Define the type of illustration. Is it a photo, a film still, an emoji, a gif, a meme, a cartoon etc?
- What are the illustrations showing?
- How are illustrations used to transport meaning?

	type of illustration (photo, gif, emoji, cartoon, film still ...)?	**What does it show?**	**Why is it used? What is the meaning?**
1. p. 4			

c) Find more examples and add them to the list.

d) CHALLENGE Describe the layout of words and the way some words are written. What could be the reason people use such a layout?

e) CHALLENGE There are parts in the play where the TL seems to intersect with the IRL, e.g. pictures are shown IRL (pp. 22, 34, 45, 71-73). What could be the playwright's intention?

Putting the play on stage

22

The director of a play decides how elements of the play script can be transferred to the stage.

a) **Group work** Come up with an option for how TL can be staged. Consider how light, sound, actors, stage and audience can play a role.

b) Watch the video of a scene from a production and note down how TL is staged. Explain the effect on the audience. You can find a link to the video here: **Webcode** DSW-73685-18

c) Take a look at the production photos from the version staged at the Royal Court theatre in London in 2021. Considering the elements on stage (cables, purple-blue cloud, dark background) and the actors' gestures, what part of the play could be shown? You can find a link to the photo gallery here: **Webcode** DSW-73685-19

VIPs

23

Cleo and Kara are making references to various famous people existing in IRL.

Joanne The Scammer | Cardi B | Angela Davis | Maxine Water | MLK | Saartjie (Sarah Baartman)

a) **Group work** Placemat: Get into groups using the placemat method:
- Each member finds out about one historical figure.
- Write your findings into your section of the placemat.
- Turn the placemat clockwise so that you can read your teammates' findings.
- Discuss and agree on a result, which you write into the group section in the middle.
- Present your results in front of the class.

b) Discuss: To what extent are these people important for the context of the play?

Body images

24

a) CHOOSE Choose a country: Iran, Japan, New Zealand, Brazil, France, Kenya, South Korea, Mauritania, Oman or United States and prepare a two minute talk on the beauty standard of this country as it is described in the video "How Beauty standards differ around the world". You can find a link to the video here: **Webcode** DSW-73685-20

Info

Body image

Body image refers to a person's emotional attitudes, beliefs, and perceptions of their own body. [...]
Body image relates to
- what a person believes about their appearance
- how they feel about their body, height, weight, and shape
- how they sense and control their body as they move

A person's body image will range from positive, or satisfaction with their body, to negative, or dissatisfaction with their body.

b) Who defines what beauty is? Explain the following quote in the context of body image as it is described in the info box:
"[...] and even Miss Fitzgerald always said how pretty your hair was, and the only time she came remotely close to commenting on how nice my hair was, was when my Mum straightened it for the Year 5 pictures." (p. 35)

25 **Pair work**

Now take a look at the following photo by Carrie Mae Weems of a woman in front of a mirror. You can find a link here: **Webcode** **DSW-73685-21**. What does she want to show the viewer about black body image / ethnic identity? Explain.

a) Read the quote by Jasmine Lee-Jones.

> I keep a scrapbook with pictures for everything that I write. The main image is currently [art by Carrie Mae Weems] of a black woman looking in the mirror saying "Mirror, mirror on the wall, who's the fairest of them all?" and the mirror's response is "Snow White, you black bitch." That's very much this play.

Elements and structure of a play

26

a) Label the following elements of a play script: stage directions, scene, characters, title, setting, playwright, text and cast.

Seven methods of killing Kylie Jenner ← 1. ______________

by Jasmine Lee-Jones ← 2. ______________

← 3. ______________

Cleo a.k.a @INCOGNEGRO | Leanne Henlon
Kara | Tia Bannon ← 4. ______________

1. ← 5. ______________

5th March 2019 4:01 AM ← 6. ______________
The bird expands and suddenly we are on Twitter.

.... ← 7. ______________

Suddenly a figure enters lurking. She creeps on CLEO; touches her.
[...]

KARA: (*in a roadman lilt.*) Fuck are you on blad! ← 8. ______________

b) Normally, the development of the plot follows a certain structure as shown below.
- Does the play meet this scheme?
- Where can you see contemporary elements?

Tip You can find an explanation of the different terms in *Camden Town Oberstufe* on page 350.

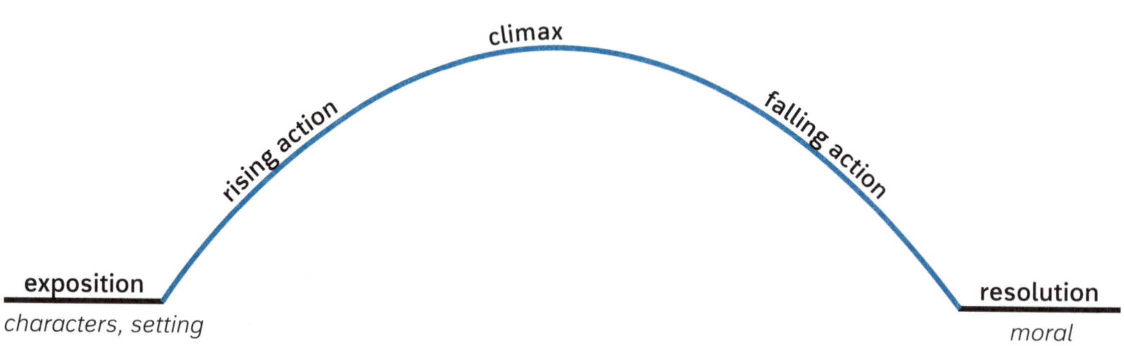

Reviews

27 → **Language support** Writing a film review, p. 116

a) Lee-Jones created a contemporary theatre play that has been widely reviewed. Compare the two opinions by Kate Wywer (1.) and Natasher Beecher (2.).

→ **Language support** Comparing, p. 16

1. Although the physicalisation of the internet is imaginative, the Twitter-interlude structure feels a little trapped towards the end, as if it's stopped inventing. The arguments begin to circle and the finale can't quite hold the weight of history it attempts to. Nevertheless, Henlon and Bannon are gripping throughout. Jones is a brilliant, dynamic writer, and this is a striking debut.

2. For us black women '*Seven methods of killing kylie Jenner*' with its blend of nostalgia and heart, is us being seen and being heard in a way that's almost too difficult to watch, our collective trauma laid bare. [...]

   For anyone who isn't black, and white people, in particular, this play will resonate with you in a magical way that you won't quite understand. But one thing is for sure, this poignant play that goes beyond just the zeitgeist is for everyone. It's a play for now and for after – a cultural marker of the way the world is changing and needs to change. Everyone should go see it.

b) CHOOSE

Write a review as a tweet.

OR

Write a review for a broadsheet newspaper.

The influence of social media on young people's identity

1

a) **Pair work** Brainstorming: list advantages and disadvantages of using social media.
b) Explain the chart. → **S18** How to analyse statistics → **Language support** Analyzing tables, graphs and charts, p. 101

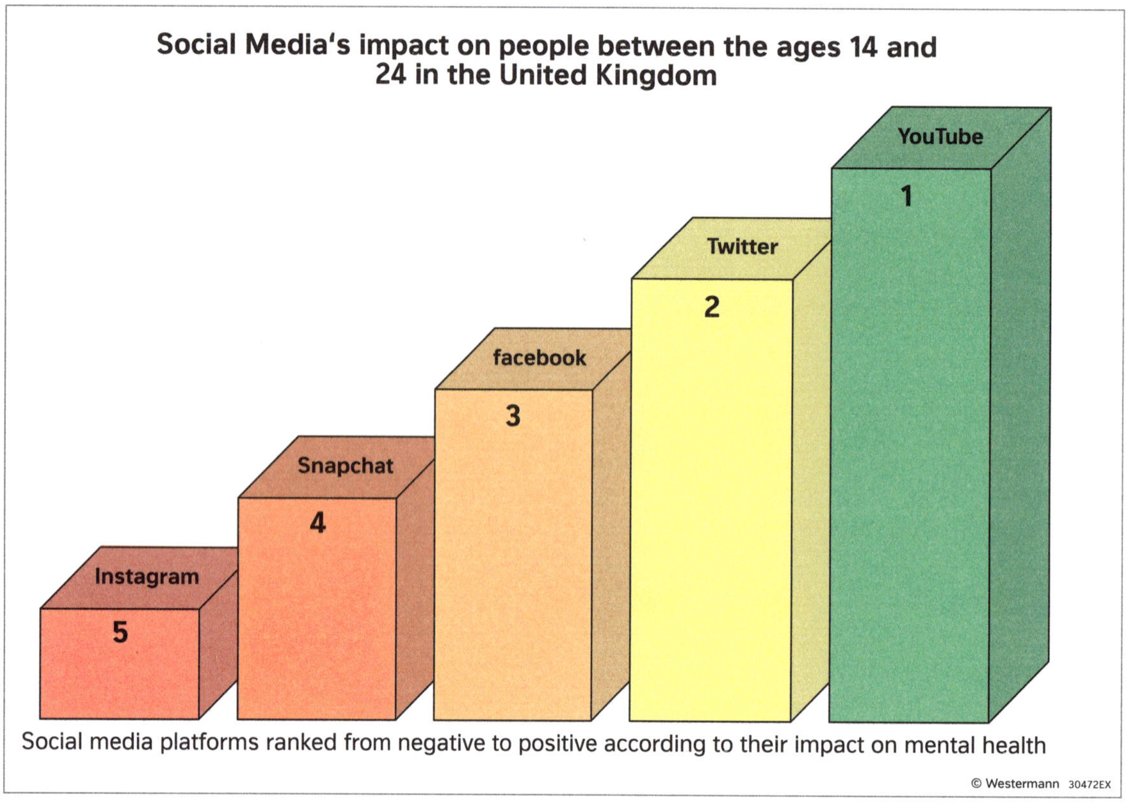

c) **Pair work** Discuss: Would you take part in a school challenge of a social media free week?

2

Tweets play a major role in *seven methods of killing kylie jenner* and are responsible for the play's development.

a) Examine to what extent the twitter comments are changing in the course of the play. Fill in the table with keywords.

content twitterludes	Who is writing?	scale of factual information (1 true to 9 false)	scale of humour (1 little to 9 the most)	scale of hatred (1 little to 9 the most)
1				
2				

content twitterludes	Who is writing?	scale of factual information (1 true to 9 false)	scale of humour (1 little to 9 the most)	scale of hatred (1 little to 9 the most)
3				
4				
5				
6				
7				
8				
9				
10				
11				

b) Choose from the following adjectives to describe the development: use a timeline / graph / colour scheme to illustrate.

accusing | amused | conspirational | funny | homophobic | inflammatory | international | irritated | misogynist | racist | sexist | shocked | surprised

c) With the increasing usage of digital technologies, a new form of bullying has emerged: "cyberbullying". Have you or your friends ever experienced cyberbullying? Illustrate (topics, feelings, consequences).

d) **Pair work** At what point in the development of the twitterludes do you think cyberbullying starts? Give reasons.

3

Cleo and Kara are having a discussion about the reactions to the death threats against Cleo that are announced in TL (pp. 43-44).

a) List their arguments. Give your opinion.

b) Cleo describes the following humiliating incident. What is happening?

"Cameras flashing without my consent
Over and over
Images posted all over socials
Me a meme
A silent, unconsenting gif
Like I was some sort of spectacle
Or a fucking freak
I've never felt so ugly in my life." (p. 48)

c) Taking photos – now and fifty years ago: what has changed? What role does social media play today compared to then? → **Language support** Comparing, p. 16

d) Internet research: Find out about the rules of taking photographs in public and private areas in Germany.

The role of ethnic identity on (social) media

4

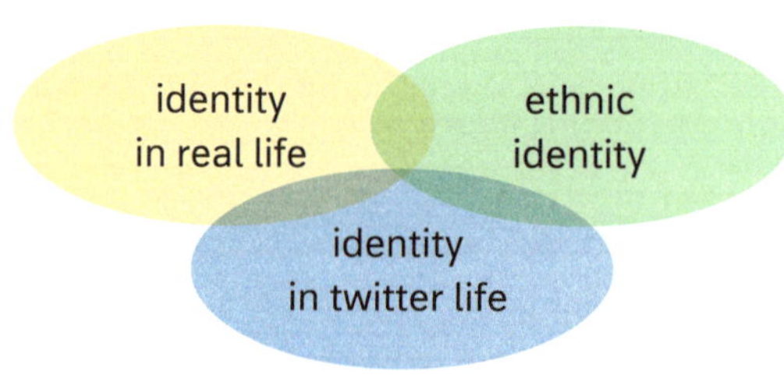

a) Cleo is a black woman having an identity in real life and in twitter life ("incognegro") and for both identities, her ethnic identity seems to play a role. How are these identities connected?

b) CHOOSE Take one of the quotes concerning the topic "skin colour" and explain it in the context of the conversation between Cleo and Kara.

- "You don't own blackness just because you're dark-skinned!" (p. 37)

OR

- "You are a lightie" (p. 33)

OR

- "All the BW considered universally beautiful are lighties" (p. 34)

Stating your opinion

5 → **S6** How to write a discussion / comment → **S9** How to structure a text → **S8** How to improve your text

Cleo shows her anger by creating hypothetical death threats to Kylie Jenner.

a) CHOOSE

Write a comment on the question of whether you think social media is a good channel to state your opinion.

OR

Pair work Write an electronic text together with a partner in a collaborative document.

> **Help** Alternative options to state your opinion and make it public:
> - going on a strike
> - talking to people face-to-face
> - sending emails or letters to the government
> - starting a petition

b) Why did the playwright choose to include twitter in her play?

MEDIATION

6 → **S19** How to improve your mediation skills

a) Read the article.

b) Write an email to the playwright Jasmine Lee-Jones in which you describe the latest development in Germany concerning the influence of social media on politics. Refer to her play by pointing out parallels.

Anfeindungen gegen Sarah-Lee Heinrich
Medienexpertin: Koordinierte Twitter-Kampagnen als Methode

Immer häufiger werden Akteure aus Politik und Medien im Netz mit fragwürdigen Aussagen aus ihrer Vergangenheit konfrontiert. Dabei gerate aus dem Blick, aus welchen Kreisen diese Enthüllungen stammen, sagte Tajana Graovac vom „No Hate Speech Movement“ im Dlf.

The German politician Sarah-Lee Heinrich

Ein paar Tweets können reichen, damit bei Twitter und darüber hinaus innerhalb weniger Stunden eine große Debatte in Gang kommt. So war das zuletzt zum Beispiel im Fall der neuen Bundessprecherin der Grünen Jugend.

Sarah-Lee Heinrich geriet in den Fokus wegen mehrerer alter Nachrichten, in denen sie im Jahr 2015 zum Beispiel „Heil“ unter einen Tweet mit Hakenkreuz geschrieben hatte. Die heute 20-Jährige schrieb, sie könne sich nicht daran erinnern, als Jugendliche jemals einen solchen Tweet abgesetzt zu haben.„Das war maximal dumm und unangebracht“, schrieb Heinrich. Die Sozialwissenschafts-Studentin betonte aber auch, dass sie sich „jetzt nicht zu allem erklären“ wolle, „was ich mal so mit 14 gedacht und gesagt habe“.

Erst Tweets, dann Morddrohungen

Heinrich beklagte außerdem, seit ihrer Wahl versuchten Rechte, Shitstorms gegen sie hochzuziehen: „Haben wohl Bammel vor einer schwarzen, linken Frau“, schrieb Heinrich. Nach diesen Tweets zog sich Heinrich vorerst aus der Öffentlichkeit zurück. Der Grünen-Jugendorganisation zufolge hatte sie Mord- und Gewaltandrohungen erhalten. Es gehe „jetzt erst einmal darum, alles für ihre Sicherheit zu tun“, sagte der scheidende Bundessprecher der Grünen Jugend, Georg Kurz.

„Das ist koordiniert“

Dass der Fall eine solche Entwicklung genommen hat, sei typisch, sagte Tajana Graovac vom „No Hate Speech Movement“ im Deutschlandfunk „Was wir feststellen können, dass es große Accounts sind, die meistens eher in der rechten Ecke zu finden sind, die große Reichweite haben“, sagte Graovac.

Accounts aus rechten und rechtsextremen Kreisen würden dann dafür sorgen, dass sich die entsprechenden Nachrichten weit verbreiten. „Das ist koordiniert. Und es ist tatsächlich auch immer das gleiche Schema und das geht fast immer nach der gleichen Dynamik“, so Graovac weiter.

Manipulierte Kampagnen erkennen
Zudem würden zum Teil Screenshots verbreitet, die nachträglich manipuliert worden seien. „Man schneidet die Zeit und das Datum ab, damit die irgendwie auch aktuell aussehen. Es werden teilweise Wörter weggelassen, damit die Tweets noch schlimmer klingen. Und das zieht dann wirklich Kreise." Aufgabe von Journalistinnen und Journalisten sei es, dies zu erkennen und nicht auf eine Kampagne hereinzufallen. Sie müssten offenlegen, „dass es eine gezielte, koordinierte Attacke ist gegen eine schwarze Person".

Cartoon analysis – images of black female identity

7 → **S17** How to work with cartoons

a) Study the woman's depiction in the cartoon carefully, then describe it.

b) Explain the cartoon's message by referring to its individual elements.

c) Come up with a possible title and give reasons for your decision.

Language support
index finger | megaphone | speech bubble

d) Black women are regularly depicted in the media and society as 'angry', 'aggressive' and 'sassy'. Imagine in which situations black women could be seen as behaving in an "angry" way?

e) Read the following Wikipedia entry on this stereotype. You can find a link to the text here: **Webcode** DSW-73685-22.

Pair work

- Sum up the text in keywords and compare your result with a partner.

f) Discuss how it is possible for black women to escape the vicious circle of being referred to as an "angry black woman" when they show anger about being called this term.
You may refer to M. Obama's reactions described in the following newspaper excerpt:

Michelle Obama: 'I'm no angry black woman'

The Obamas, by New York Times reporter Jodi Kantor, portrays her as a behind-the-scenes force in the White House.

[...] Mrs Obama did not deny being an important voice to her husband.

"I am his biggest ally," Mrs Obama said. "I am one of his biggest confidants. But he has dozens of really smart people who surround him. That's not to say that we don't have discussions and conversations."

"I guess it's more interesting to imagine this conflicted situation here and a strong woman. But that's been an image that people have tried to paint of me since the day Barack announced [he would run for president] – that I'm some angry black woman," she said.

"I just try to be me. And my hope is that over time people get to know me," she told CBS. "And they get to judge me for me." [...]

8

a) Read the article.

b) Outline Ritu Prasad's view on the myth of the "angry black woman" as presented in this article.

____

____

____

Serena Williams and the trope[1] of the 'angry black woman'

by Ritu Prasad

Mammies, jezebels, Sapphires. Black women in America have long been dogged by negative stereotypes, rooted in a history of racism and slavery. In the aftermath of Serena Williams' controversial US Open loss, it's the trope of the "angry black woman" that has once again re-emerged.

During the US Open final, Williams received a code violation for coaching[2], a penalty point for breaking her racquet and a game penalty for calling the umpire a "thief". And later, a fine of $17,000 (£13,000).

Her reactions to the referee's calls – which the Women's Tennis Association has since decri[b]ed as "sexist" – were no different from how many top players react in the heat of a championship game.

But it was the way she was punished for her anger that has sparked further outrage.

[...] The law professor and tennis fan Prof Trina Jones has studied racial stereotyping and how it plays into the lives of African-American women.

"Black women are not supposed to push back and when they do, they're deemed to be domineering. Aggressive. Threatening. Loud." Similar words have been levelled at[3] Serena Williams more than once, as well as former First Lady Michelle Obama and top Democrat Maxine Waters in recent years.

Prof Jones says some have compared the referee's calls to speeding tickets: many people speed and sometimes a few are caught. But that analogy, she says, misses the point that African Americans are disproportionately pulled aside. In the case of Williams, she was first dinged[4] on a coaching violation that happens often but is rarely called out as the player's fault. "Why would a black woman in a championship match therefore be called on it?" Prof Jones says, adding that an attack on one's integrity is only natural to be angry about. "[Williams] is outraged because she knows the context."

The myth of the 'angry black woman'

The "angry black woman" trope has its roots in 19th Century America, when minstrel shows, which

Annotations

[1] **trope** = *Tropus, bildlicher Ausdruck*

[2] **Coaching** = Players aren't allowed to be coached in Grand Slam matches. Violations lead to warnings or penalties.

[3] to **be levelled at** = thrown at / labels given to her without much consideration or thought

[4] to **be dinged** = sharp riging sound; here: held to account

Annotations

[5] **comic skit** = a comedy sketch
[6] **sassy** = *frech*
[7] **pervasive** = common
[8] **grapple** = to fight with or to continually discuss a difficult issue
[9] **clarion call** = appeal

involved comic skits[5] and variety acts, mocking African Americans became popular. Blair Kelley, associate professor of history at North Carolina State University, says black women were often played by overweight white men who painted their faces black and donned fat suits "to make them look less than human, unfeminine, ugly". "Their main way of interacting with the men around them was to scream and fight and come off angry, irrationally so, in response to the circumstances around them," she says. "The real problem in their everyday life was not the structural things that black people faced, but the mouth of the black woman – her tone, her irrationality and her anger," Prof Kelley says of Sapphire's role.

As segregation laws known as Jim Crow laws saw black Americans assaulted, jailed and killed, popular culture pushed ideas of "sassy[6] mammies" and "Sapphires" – an archetype depicting black women with iron-fists, yelling at everyone from children to white men. [...] This trope of the "angry black woman" has endured, and has been pervasive[7] in modern media even without more overtly racist portrayals, says Brandi Collins, senior campaign director at the racial justice organisation Color of Change.

On screen, it is easy to push sass for laughs. But black women in America see these depictions translate differently in real life. For Ms Collins, the picture of the "hyperemotional" black woman has become more commonplace as Americans grapple[8] with issues of polarised politics and civility. Black women, she says, are often faced with people responding to their emotions "from a place of perceived fear. There's almost a paranoia around it. A feeling that you have to go above and beyond to make people feel comfortable around you."

Robin Boylorn, an intercultural communications professor at the University of Alabama told the BBC it seems impossible to be a black woman and not be angry, after "generations of oppression, discrimination and erasure". "Black women should be celebrated for not being completely consumed by anger," she says.

"Men are allowed to be angry as a performance of masculinity. White women are allowed to be angry as a clarion call[9]. So black women should be encouraged to express their anger as well, particularly in the face of injustice."

[...] Ms Collins notes that fixing the problem is not just about eliminating the "angry black woman" trope. "For every type of white man you can imagine, there's a movie about his story and his experience and his journey. Black women in media aren't afforded that diversity of experience," she says. Instead, understanding the diversity of a black woman's experience – and not just her anger – is the key.

For Williams, that's a lesson she hopes her fans will learn from her US Open upset. "I'm here to fight for women's rights and women's equality. The fact that I have to go through this is an example," she told reporters after the match. "Maybe it didn't work out for me, but it's going to work out for the next person."

9

Explain why it is inadequate to refer to an African American woman as an "angry black woman".

Looking back at the play

10

Pair work Cleo is being criticized for her behaviour in the TL, e.g. "I for one can't believe @INCOGNEGRO acting like dis. U ain't the next civil rights activist." (p. 19).

Are there any more parallels between Serena Williams' depiction as an angry woman and the comments in TL that describe Cleo as hysterical and over-reacting?

11

Group work Your school is planning a project week with the topic "school for the future" and is asking students to send in podcasts, videos, posters, etc. with ideas of how schools can address and eliminate racism. What would be your contribution?